sweet hell on fire

*a memoir of the prison I worked in
and the prison I lived in*

sara lunsford

sourcebooks

Published by Sourcebooks, Inc.
P.O. Box 4410, Naperville, Illinois 60567-4410
(630) 961-3900
Fax: (630) 961-2168
www.sourcebooks.com

Library of Congress Cataloging-in-Publication Data

Lunsford, Sara.
  Sweet hell on fire : a memoir of the prison I worked in and the prison I lived
in / Sara Lunsford.
     pages cm
  Includes bibliographical references and index.
  (paperback : alkaline paper) 1. Lunsford, Sara. 2. Women correctional person-
nel—United States—Biography. 3. Correctional personnel—United States—
Biography. 4. Workaholics—United States—Biography. 5. Alcoholics—United
States—Biography. 6. Job stress—United States—Case studies. 7. Prisons—
United States—Case studies. 8. Male prisoners—United States—Case studies.
9. Violent offenders—United States—Case studies. I. Title.
  HV9468.L86A3 2012
  365'.33—dc23
  [B]
                                        2012030926

Printed and bound in the United States of America.
                    VP 10 9 8 7 6 5 4 3 2 1

For Jonathan.
My white knight, my alpha hero, and my Happily Ever After.

And for my dad.

acknowledgments

THIS BOOK WOULDN'T HAVE BEEN POSSIBLE WITHOUT THE fierce belief in me and the story I had to tell from my wonderful agent and friend, Deidre Knight, and my fantastic editor, Shana Drehs.

Or without my critique partner, Jennifer L. Hart, who held my hand when I had to relive some of the darkest memories, or the rest of the divas: Gail Reinhart and Traci Poff just for being themselves.

Angelee Van Allman, for being one of the most amazing, positive, loving people I've ever known.

Big thanks also to Jamie Brenner, who also believed I had a story to tell.

Last, but not least, every officer who lives the world between these pages every day to keep us all safe.

Thank you!

preface

WHEN PEOPLE FIND OUT THAT I WAS A CORRECTIONS officer, they always ask for my story. They want to know what it's like behind the walls, working with inmates, if it's really like *OZ* or *Prison Break*. I'm suddenly a curious little unfamiliar bug they were surprised to find on their begonias, and they want to inspect me. It doesn't bother me, because I know the details of what we do are often kept quiet. That's just part of the culture of The Job.

Once I start talking, they always want more. And I always have more—anyone who has ever worked in law enforcement in any capacity has a million stories of the incredible, the horrible, and the obscene. It's probably not surprising, then, that I wrote the first draft of this book almost like A Girl's Guide to Prison—a manual. All stories of the prison, never anything too personal. Never anything that dug into the meat of *me*. I knew I had to dig even deeper.

So I got out my scalpel/keyboard and flayed myself open and spilled everything all over the page. Then I realized people were going to know things about me. Things I'd never told anyone else. They were going to see me at my worst, and I don't have a best to contrast it with because I'm not there yet. I'm still a work in progress.

They'd see how selfish I was, how cruel. How small.

I panicked. Why in the hell would anyone want to read about that? I was a bad mother, a bad daughter, a bad wife, a bad friend. A boozed-out, tired bar slut with no dreams and no future.

But I was a good officer.

That mollified me temporarily...I could live with people not liking the person I was. Or even the person I am. Whatever.

But I'd be showing everyone my soft, sticky insides. The things that hurt me, the things that made me bleed. The things that still sometimes rise up in the dark and choke me. My weakness. It twists up my guts even now, but like the old adage says, in for a penny, in for a pound, right?

Any book is a type of voyeurism—you're looking into other worlds that live in someone else's head, or you're looking into someone else's life, into their thoughts. Even a how-to book is poking around in someone else's brain.

And I'd signed up to give the guided tour.

But I decided it's okay for people to look at me; in fact, I want them to, because my story could show someone else who is lost in the dark, afraid, and wondering if they'll ever see the sun again that it's still there. You can claw your way out because I'm living proof.

I'm here and living my dream. I'm a full-time writer, full-time mom, and full-time wife. Things aren't perfect, but they're damn close.

After you read my story, I hope you remember this confession at the beginning, because beginnings are always so different from endings. Beginnings are universally naïve. I won't say innocent, but they're just so far removed from the place where you emerge.

In the beginning, I had no idea that this journey would change me so much, wound me so much, or even stitch me back together as it did.

introduction

WELCOME TO MY WORLD.
I know that people frequently use this phrase in a condescending tone, but that's not the case here. My welcome is genuine and heartfelt. But you *are* going to need a map.

This book chronicles a year in my life, a year when I was working as a corrections officer for a state prison. I'd worked at the prison before, but now I was what they called a "retread." That is, I'd been dumb enough to come back for another round. The book begins near the end of the first year of my second stint—right before everything started to fall apart. And the story doesn't stop at the gate outside the walls, as if that world could be shrugged off with the uniform at the end of my shift. This is an uncensored look at the job and the effects it had on the whole of my life.

I began this year as one person but emerged on the other side quite another, both from external and internal forces. They say that during the first year of corrections, an officer is no good for The Job. After that year, they're no good for anything else. And it's true: there's very little else I'm suited for now. I write, but that's a solitary career. One in which I don't have to interact with people every day if I choose not to.

I see people differently now than I did before The Job. Still can't sit with my back to a door or eat or drink anything that's been left unattended. I look for the ulterior motive in every gesture and every kindness. I still automatically detach from most people, disengage lest I see too much of what's below the surface. I interact with men differently as well, always first seeing the predators. Except the ones who have my back—and even then, some of them are predators too. I'm working on that. I know firsthand there are good men in the world who aren't like that, but my knee-jerk reaction is to look for the animal before the man so I can protect myself.

Which brings me to the most difficult thing about doing The Job. It wasn't The Job itself. It was how it infected everything else like some alien virus. Officers are told to be two people, to leave who they become on duty behind the walls at the exit gate, as if they can shrug off that skin—that face—and forget all the horrors the human animal is capable of inflicting. The darkness invades everything it touches on a cellular level, and no amount of scrubbing will get it clean. The brutality of the environment changed me, made me stronger, harder—tested my mettle—and in some ways forged it too. As Nietzsche said, "He who fights with monsters might take care lest he thereby become a monster."

But you're going to have a map, so you're not going to get lost like I did.

It is as follows:

The prison where I worked has the capacity to house approximately 2,300 inmates and was composed of four custody levels: Special Management (Segregation), Maximum, Medium, and Minimum, spread across two units. There are eight cell houses in the Max, four in the Medium, and four in the Minimum. The Special Management, or Segregation, unit is contained inside the Maximum unit and, along with the Medium, makes up the Central unit. These are often referred to as the Max, or the Medium. The Minimum unit is self-contained and often called "The Hill" or East unit, as it sits across the highway and up on a lovely rise. In the spring, it doesn't even look like prison. There's landscaping with trees and flowers and picnic tables. It's softer. It's probably not surprising that it used to be a women's unit (which was moved to another part of the state). Although, that's faulty logic, because any officer who has worked with both women and men will tell you the women are tougher, meaner, and harder to handle.

The Max is the oldest part of the prison, and the original part of the structure looks almost like a castle. The architecture never failed to impress me every time I pulled into the parking lot. The Medium is more modern, with cell houses that are more like dormitories than anything else.

An inmate's classification, or custody level, is determined by his crime and how much time he has left to do. The harder, more violent offenders are in the Max, but they can earn privileges to go to the Medium unit where they have more freedom of movement.

The prison is its own little town. It has a water treatment facility, fire station on-site outside the walls, private industry— manufacturing plants that contract with the state and function on-site, the lower level positions staffed by inmates—cafeteria, and medical clinics. A gas station, an auto garage, a machine shop. There are roads and libraries, a post office, a chapel, and even some livestock.

It also has a death chamber that isn't currently in use.

The prison is more than a hundred years old, and back when it was first built, it didn't have a death chamber. It had gallows and a wall where the condemned faced a firing squad. That part of the prison is still there. It's now where the inmates have their rec or yard time.

The prison runs on three shifts. First shift begins early and runs six to two, second is two to ten, and third is ten to six. Officers don't get a lunch hour. You eat at your desk, if there's time. Each shift has its own particular reputation. Six to two is the shift with most of the brass, or supervisors, the old-timers. Two to ten is the animal house shift, all the party people work that shift. And ten to six has the reputation of being lazy because there's less inmate movement—that happens on the two to ten. For all the idiocy that happens on the second shift, that's the one that gets stuck with most of the bitch work.

Rank and chain of command run almost like the military. Corporal—also known as Corrections Officer I or COI— is the bottom of the rung. I started here. The next step up is Sergeant—Corrections Officer II or COII. Then we have First Sergeant, or Corrections Specialist I or CSI. Above that roll Lieutenant, Captain, Major, Associate Warden, Warden, and then the Secretary of Corrections. The Captain is generally responsible for everything that happens on shift; the Lieutenants aid the Captains, First Sergeants are responsible for their sergeants and cell houses, and the Sergeants for their individual cell houses and Corporals.

Everything occurs on a schedule in prison. There's a time to sleep, a time to be counted, a time to exercise, a time to read, pray, bathe, eat, and there are even restrictions on when you can take care of the most basic of bodily functions.

Even for the officers. Job assignments happen at three different times: once a year at rotation, where everyone moves posts (or assignments), after promotion, or if hired for a specialty post. There are regular posts, which means the position is the same five days a week, or relief posts, in which the officer splits time between different positions. Some officers choose to be unassigned and work wherever they're needed.

I could drone on about more technical things, sketch a more detailed map, but it would cloud the path. I have a manual full of rules, regulations, laws, an inmate handbook, an officer's handbook, but all of that is just words on paper. It's the situations, the action in the real life that show this underworld as it is.

The training, the practical information, the technical jargon—it's all important. But it's nothing like living it.

Sara Lunsford

day 1

THERE IS NO STAIN REMOVER IN THE WORLD THAT WILL get human brain matter out of a poly-cotton blend.

It looks just like they portray it in slasher flicks and gore fests, like some weird lumpy gray sausage straining to get out of its dull casing. There's blood too. A contrast so stark it seems like someone took a red Sharpie to an old noir movie. Everything fades to the background and all you can see is the red. It sears into your line of sight brighter than the sun so when you close your eyes, it's still there—burning hot.

I didn't think about the red and the gray—the blood and the brains—until hours after the first time I saw them spread out before me. Not until I was at home and my uniform pants were splayed out across the washer and I looked at my pretreaters and stain removers, then back at the strange slashes of rusted red.

When it happened, there was no time for reflection, for horror or shock. Only action. Only what my training had prepared me for.

A man on his back in the yard.

Even without the crimson spray on the concrete, I knew he was dead. Prison is the lowest common denominator of civilization, where primal instincts and base needs rule. It's a place where showing soft underbelly to the other predators is a sign of weakness. For a man to be on his back out on the yard where everyone could see him, his belly exposed, he had to be dead.

Especially with a bloody sock on the ground next to him. Nothing says "pay me" to the rest of your customers like a lock in a sock to the back of the head of someone who *didn't* pay. I broke into a run before the alarm came over the radio. First responders erupted from the cell houses and other posts they were working, filling the yard like so many soldier ants ready for duty.

I wasn't the first one on the scene, but it was me on my knees in the gore assisting the officer who began CPR. Pieces of the inmate's skull were scattered on the ground like broken bits of china, and his head looked like a rotten watermelon. Rescue breaths, CPR, and all the emergency care in the world couldn't help him.

The memory is stark and faded at the same time, parts of it as if they happened yesterday and other parts like they never happened at all. I know EMS was called, I know I filled out stacks of paperwork, but I don't remember it. I don't remember talking to anyone, or doing anything that day. All I remember is the hard concrete under my knees and the blood on my hands, beneath my fingernails. The gray bits on my pants of what used to be a person.

Everything about him that made his place in the world was in that fleshy mess. The bad. His crime, the pain he inflicted on others, his motivations to do violence. The good. The people he loved. His hopes, his dreams. His memories. Everything that made him what he was right there under the afternoon sun spread out for any who cared to look.

I remember wiping my hands on my pants, the red and gray smearing up my thighs when I stood. Then I was at home, doing my laundry and wondering how the hell I was supposed to get a stain like that out of my uniform and if he'd been positive for HIV or HEP-C. There was a good chance of both—he'd been a punk. The tattoo on his neck marked him as Blood property, a commodity to be bought and sold, or rented out as the gang deemed fit. Add to that the infected injection site on his arm where he'd been shooting up, and he was two for two. Unprotected sex and needle sharing.

Even that realization was distant and unreal at the time. The only thing that was real was that I had been wrist deep in meat that used to be a man.

Shout got the blood out, but the gray remained.

day 2

"FUCK YOU, FATASSCUNTBITCH," THE INMATE SLURRED around crooked teeth that reminded me of the bared and gnarled roots of an old weeping willow bleached out in the sun.

Fuck me? No, buddy. Fuck *you*. "Yeah, fuck me. Whatever, man. Cuff up," I said, bored with the exchange already and indicating he should present his wrists to be handcuffed. I didn't need this after what had happened on the yard the day before.

But the inmate hadn't come out of his cell for a week. He hadn't showered; he hadn't come out to go to chow, hadn't come out for yard. He was either afraid of someone or hiding some serious contraband. Most guys were always ready, willing, and able to come out of their cells for anything that could get them there.

I mean *anything*. The price of Madagascarian intestinal fly larvae rose by a quarter of a cent? They had to get out of their cells to call their mothers who invest in that sort of thing, and if they didn't, said sainted mothers would lose their homes. The moon was full so it was their turn to scrub the lint out of their bellybuttons with a special tool they only have in the clinic and…The reason didn't matter. Out was out.

This guy wanted no part of anything.

I could tell from the way he narrowed his eyes and the hard set to his jaw he was taking my measure and deciding how far he could push me.

I sighed heavily. "Look, I don't give a damn when you do it, but you will do it. If not for me, then for the blacksuits." I shrugged. Blacksuits was another name for our special teams. Not exactly SWAT, but they were the big guns who dealt with combative inmates and other emergencies. They could come hand him his ass on a platter. I'd gain compliance one way or another.

The inmate leaned toward the toilet and shoved something in the bowl.

"Don't do it! Do not flush that—" I didn't even get the command out before he'd tried to flush whatever contraband he didn't want me to find.

Good thing I'd turned off the water to his cell before I'd confronted him.

"You bitch," he shrieked when the toilet didn't flush.

Your mom, asshole. Of course I didn't say it. They could call us every filthy name in the book and we had to take it, but we weren't allowed to insult their mothers. Because it gave them "rage issues." Whatever. What kind of pussy can dish it out but can't take it? Oh, right. It's prison.

But I'm a professional. So I kept my comments to myself.

Even when he whipped his dick out and pissed all over his cell. The arc of urine sprayed his walls, his desk, his bunk, and the pile of clothes in the corner. I had this sinking feeling in my gut he was going to try to spray me too.

"Good luck, bitch." He turned, the stream of piss arching ever closer to me.

He could piss on his own things; that's why we have gloves. But *on* me? *Oh, hell no.* "Rack the door!" I called down the run to the other officer on the tier, telling him to open the inmate's door. He'd be pissing in a bag when I was done with him.

The cell door dragged open, the mechanism slow and

plodding, creaking like an old man's knees. He let go of his dick and it hung there out of his state-issued boxers like a shriveling sausage. All color drained out of his face in tandem with the dwindling stream of urine. He hadn't expected me to open the door.

"Now what?" I'd launch myself into the cell to gain his compliance if I had to, but if I could get it done without touching him that was better for everyone involved.

To my surprise, he turned around and faced the wall. He put his arms behind his back, showing he was ready to be handcuffed. I locked the cuffs into place quickly, careful to make sure I kept my own stance balanced and a good distance between us. Should he have decided to fight, he wouldn't have the advantage.

"I didn't think you'd open the door, Sarge," he said this under his breath.

Yeah, they never do. Lots of officers make a big show of threatening to rack the door, to let the inmate out to make good on his threats and the officer to make good on his, but they don't. The inmate keeps talking shit, the officer keeps talking shit, and it's just a bunch of posturing—and more shit. Males circling each other's territory, waving their dicks around. I didn't have a dick to wave around, so I had no room to posture. I could only make him feel like I'd slapped him with someone else's dick, rode him hard, and put him away wet.

I hauled him out onto the run and directed him down to the office. Catcalls echoed throughout the cell house, calling him a pussy for cuffing up, calling me alternatively a badass and a bitch for cuffing him. A couple of guys even mooed at me, but that wasn't anything new.

Even on my first day, when we took the tour, I heard animal

sounds and whispers of, "That's a big bitch." You got that right, motherfucker. Don't forget it.

Down in the office the Officer in Charge (OIC) gave me a stern look, his old jowls shaking with his displeasure. "Why'd you wind them up?"

A guy pissed all over his cell, wouldn't come out to shower, called me every name in the book, and *I'd* wound them up?

"Had to be done." I shrugged.

"I heard them mooing at you. You can't take it out on them because you're fat. You need a thicker skin."

My jaw almost fell off my face it dropped so fast. "Right. Let's look at this again. A targeted search of an inmate's cell because it hasn't been searched in weeks coupled with the inmate's unusual behavior makes me doing my job some sad, fat-girl vendetta?" I stopped and turned around, trying to look at my own ass. I looked back up at the OIC, incredulous. "Well, fuck me. Where did that come from? I went to bed skinny and woke up fat." I rolled my eyes, and the other officer in the room clamped his mouth shut and buried his head in his arms on the desk as he shook with laughter. "I know what I look like and I don't care what they think of me. Or you for that matter."

He looked at me. "You're a woman. Of course you do."

I'd forgotten this guy believed that because I had a vagina, I wasn't capable of concerning my little head with anything beyond my next pair of shoes and what I should make my man for dinner.

I really didn't care what the inmates thought of me. For someone's opinion to matter, you have to give a shit about them. You have to care for someone's words to hurt you. Some snaggle-toothed, illiterate ghetto rat doesn't like looking at my ass? I'm certainly not going to cry about it. A thicker skin? I have an outer shell like the tiles of the space shuttle. Further, if I did care, that would mean I wanted to be attractive to the inmate.

Yeah, I'd rather gargle with razor blades, thank you very much.

I got on the PA system. "Attention in the cell house. The OIC is irritated by your barnyard sounds. I, however, find them amusing. But Mamma already knows what sounds the cow makes. Can anyone tell me what sound a horse makes?"

The cell house erupted in laughter, breaking the tension that had been building from the interaction between me and the inmate. Whenever something like that went down, it was never just about the officer and the inmate. So keeping a situation at the lowest level of escalation was important.

He snatched it away from me. "This isn't your cell house, little girl. You can't just come in here and—"

"And what?" I snatched it back. "I can't come in here and do my job? Why don't you give it to me in writing that you told me not to search cells?"

His mouth hung open, a rusty hinge swaying back and forth in the wind. He couldn't say anything to that. Some of the old-timers were tired and didn't like to upset the status quo. But I wasn't an old-timer and wasn't tired. Whatever the inmate had hidden was something he wasn't supposed to have. There were reasons for rules and reasons things were contraband. I was looking out for my fellow officers by getting that crap out of population. I was looking out for the inmates too.

I was also building a reputation. Fair. Firm. Consistent. Not only was that my training, it's what worked. Reputations are like trust. Hard to build, easy to shatter, and it doesn't matter what the truth of the situation happens to be, only how the others perceive it.

Women have to be harder in this environment. We're seen

as the weak link by both officers and inmates until we prove otherwise. Something as simple as doing my job went a long way for a solid reputation.

Later, when I followed through searching his cell, I found the contraband he'd tried to hide. Not only did he have a baggie of weed under the clothes he'd pissed on, but he also had a joint in the toilet.

But that wasn't the important find.

The important one was the seven steel rods that had been stolen from the metal-working shop and taped underneath his cell door.

He was making shanks.

I'd done the right thing demanding to search his cell. I also knew I was lucky he hadn't gone for one of those steel rods and put it through my face when I'd ordered his door opened.

After what had happened in the yard, it was also a sign that the shit was about to get deep.

day 3

Work seemed unnaturally quiet, and while I was sure something big was brewing, I admitted it could be just another day.

Nothing happened. Everyone went home safe. That made it a good day above everything else.

But there was no rest for the wicked.

My husband and I had separated almost a year ago, and I lived with my parents. That hadn't been an ideal situation at seventeen, let alone at thirty. I loved my parents, but we had different ideas about how I should live my life and how I should raise my children. I appreciated their input, they're fantastic to my kids, but ultimately, I didn't want their advice unsolicited.

My mother had been so angry when I took "The Job." I'd had another job offer from an airline the same time the offer from the prison came, but my car had a catastrophic blowout and I had to accept the job at the prison. I could get rides in town, but all the way to the airport was another matter entirely. She told me she'd spent twenty years worrying if my father was going to come home every night working at the federal prison, and now she had to worry about me at the state prison and it was a shitty thing for me to do to her.

My dad acted differently. He asked me if I had all the equipment I needed to start. He told me I would see people carrying these huge Maglite flashlights so they could use them like billy clubs, but that I shouldn't take anything behind the walls I wasn't prepared to eat, meaning nothing I wouldn't want used against me or stuffed in any various orifices.

When my estranged husband caught me trying to fit my flashlight into my mouth, he asked me if I was planning on trying to promote early by showing off that I could, in fact, fit it inside.

Anyway, when I got home that night, my mother was screaming—it was a high-pitched sound, horrible and shrill, like something being torn out of her.

She was in the bedroom where she spent most of her time in those days, and all she could do was howl. The kids were spending the night with their dad and my father was at work. The dog came to me, crawling on her belly and whining, obviously afraid. This had been going on for some time.

I went into the bedroom and my mother was crying, holding her belly with vomit in the trashcan and burning cigarettes in the ashtray. She had a window open; it was summer. But she had the electric blanket wrapped around her and she was shaking.

I didn't know what to do. These attacks had been coming more often, and due to her other illnesses, she hadn't been able to leave the house so she could go see a doctor.

"Help me," she begged.

Oh, God. How? I didn't know what was wrong with her, so how could I help her?

"Help me," she cried again, louder.

I sat down on the bed next to her and tried to rub her back, to soothe her as she'd done to me when I was sick. It didn't help. Nothing did.

Her cries for help got louder until she was screaming again and I was at a loss. She screamed and screamed at me to help her and when her voice cracked, she'd whimper. All she could tell me was that it was a pain in her belly.

I called my dad and asked him to come home. He told me he would and to call an ambulance.

She screamed until they arrived, begging me the whole time to help her. To make it stop. EMS shot her up with painkillers and took her to the ER.

She spent twelve hours in the ER only to be sent home with a referral to an ob-gyn.

Still in pain and with no answers.

day 4

S HE BEGGED ME TO STAY HOME WITH HER.
But I didn't.

I couldn't.

Not only because I had no idea how to help her, but because I was still on probation at work. I could be fired for absolutely anything in the first year. If I called in sick during this time, I could lose my job. There was literally nowhere else in town I could get a job where I could get insurance and still support myself. The pay was horrible, barely a living, but the benefits were good.

My starting pay was around $12 an hour; I made approximately $24,000 a year. The poverty level guidelines for my state and a family of three sit at $27,000 a year. Incidentally, the federal average for corrections officers was $53,000 a year in 2009. I made less than half of the national average and under the poverty level.

As a kid, I'd quit so many jobs because I didn't like them, or just didn't want to do them. Like I thought they grew on trees. I'd never had a problem getting hired until I was a stay-at-home mom for eight years suddenly thrust back into the job force.

Although my husband and I were separated, and we'd had some really awful fights, he was never mean about money. He was happy to provide for his children and even gave me the money to get my own apartment.

But I couldn't keep relying on him.

The worst part was I didn't *want* to stay home with her even if I could. Honestly, I had enough shit on my plate to deal with without my mother screaming and sobbing all day long and demanding I stay in the bedroom with her while she did it.

I know, that's horrible. She's my mom. She was afraid and hurting, and she needed me. I wasn't there for her.

We didn't always have a good relationship and she was sick a lot when I was growing up. Her illnesses were due to nervous conditions. I didn't have much patience for her through those times, and I guess I thought this was the same thing. I don't know what else to say without sounding like I'm badmouthing her and making excuses. So I'll just own it. My reasons were my own, but I didn't want to do it. So I didn't.

Instead, I went to work.

I left an hour early so I had time to drive around, to ditch all my baggage at the door before I went behind the walls.

Any shit I would have carried in with me would have been twice as heavy while I was there, and I would have been distracted and maybe even a danger to my fellow officers. The inmates see those things, know to look for them.

If an officer didn't shine their boots, if their normally clean and crisp uniform was rumpled, if the way a person carried themselves was different—they'd use it to slide in. To bond. It would start out simple enough with something like: "What's wrong, Sarge? You don't look like yourself."

Do they give a shit? No. They're trying to get over on someone, have some officer cull themselves from the herd and spill their guts all over the place, telling personal business. Then suddenly he's the one who understands you, who cares about you, convinces you he's the only one…

Yeah, puke.

So I drove around with the windows down and Pantera's *Vulgar Display of Power* album as loud as it would go.

The lyrics to "Walk" have always spiked my adrenaline and amped me up, ready to go, fight or flight. In this instance, it helped me get to that constant state of alert where all corrections officers have to be to get the job done.

I dropped my baggage at the door to do my eight, then the gate, as they say.

day 5

MY FRIDAY.
 I think it was a Tuesday in the outside world, but for me, it was Friday. Last day of the workweek. Two days ahead with more bullshit, but at least it was a different flavor and I'd see my kids.

I also went out on my Friday nights. Just a couple of beers, maybe some dancing and a few games of pool. Something to decompress, to not have to be anywhere or be anything. I wasn't even going to go home and change. I'd brought my clothes with me.

Yeah, smart one that I was, I brought clothes, but no lunch. So I got a cupcake out of the vending machine.

I could have gotten a tray from the chow hall like some of the other guys I worked with, but I'd seen roaches crawl out of the trays down in Segregation. I'd accidentally jostled the cart and it looked like the tower of trays was doing the hula. Until I realized it wasn't the trays, but the roaches crawling out of them. Sadly, that wasn't specific to Segregation but the whole prison. Exterminators were in all the time, but it never seemed to do any good. All officers were advised to shake out all of their belongings before we left the institution after shift so we didn't take any of the roaches home. Anyone working there longer than five minutes probably has a roach story that would make your skin crawl right off your body.

A quiet night was too much to hope for.

Although that was my own fault.

A Segregation position was coming open soon, and I wanted it so bad I could taste it. I'd already applied for the position, but there would be a lengthy screening process with interviews and reviews of my employee file. It was a lot more work, more intense all around, but it was what I'd always thought prison should be like. It would also look great for promotions. So when I found out shift was overstaffed, I asked if I could be sent to Segregation to help out.

There was always something to do down there, even with all the inmates locked up and four officers on duty: property to be distributed or taken away, cleaning, something. I wanted to talk to the Seg OIC (First Sergeant) and show my interest in the position. I wanted him to see I could handle the job and I wouldn't cry over the bitch work all newbies get stuck with, nor would I demand he watch his mouth like some of the people who worked there and forgot they were in a prison. If you're someone who is easily offended, you don't belong working behind the walls.

The Captain asked me why in the hell I wanted to work down there. I couldn't explain it. From seeing the Seg officers' interactions with each other both inside and outside the walls, it seemed like a closer-knit group, and most everyone who worked the post promoted quickly. If this was going to be my career, I wasn't going to half-ass it; I'd go for the throat and pay my dues.

I shrugged and said it sounded fun. So he sent me and another officer down to train. The other officer was young, early twenties. He had a baby face, shoulders like a linebacker, and a mouth that wrote checks his ass could cash maybe 50 percent of the time. He'd worked Segregation before, and as we were walking to the cell house, he told me I wasn't going to get the post because he had more experience. He worked as a bouncer on his off time. Bouncing was a far cry from corrections, although a lot of the guys moonlighted as bouncers at some of the local clubs and bars.

I didn't bother to tell him this was my second stint of employment with the prison and I'd been doing this job when his mom was still wiping his ass and putting his food in a blender. I'd worked there the first time at nineteen as a single mom. I was still too young then to have the temperament to be any good at it. But now I had the experience and knew what I was doing.

"Hey, I see you finally nagged him into putting you down here," the OIC said when I walked through the extra set of doors that gave Seg an additional feeling of security.

"I've been married. I can nag the spots off a leopard."

"Yeah?" He smirked. "Why don't you go see if you can get 304 to give up his earphones? He's not supposed to have them."

"I'll give it a shot."

I didn't get a chance to try. As I passed the first cell on the lower tier, I saw that the inmate inside had a razor or some other sharp instrument. He'd cut superficial strips down his arms and had smeared blood all over himself. He'd painted his face too. He looked like something out of a Clive Barker movie. I consoled myself with the thought that at least it wasn't feces. Some of the inmates, either legitimately mentally disturbed or just looking for a diagnosis to get meds or different sentencing, would cover themselves with their own feces, make little Claymation animals out of it, or even eat it. A cutter sounded infinitely easier to deal with in my book.

"Hey, man. You okay?" I had my hand on my radio, ready to

call a medical emergency as I peered inside the darkened cell. It stank of sweat and prison food, but nothing out of the ordinary.

"Yeah," he answered. "I'm okay. You okay?" He licked his lips, slid his tongue over his teeth in a repetitive motion.

"I'm doing great, thanks for asking." My gut told me then he was just looking for a reaction, so I kept calm and cool.

"My TV has been talking to me." I relaxed the hand on my radio. In my experience, if he'd really wanted to hurt himself, he wouldn't have tried to keep me there talking.

"Oh yeah? What's it say?"

"It's just talking. Told me to cut myself."

I personally thought he was full of shit. Sounds callous, right? But not on closer inspection. His cuts were only superficial. They hadn't bled much and he'd made it a point to smear it all over himself where it was the most advantageous to being seen. I'd known girls in high school who were cutters and they'd cut deeper than that if the vending machine gave them Coke instead of Pepsi. I could cut someone deeper and with more purpose with my fingernails. I'd still be calling mental health. Protocol.

"That wasn't nice of them and it sounds distracting. You want me to take your TV so they can't talk to you anymore?"

He looked at me and narrowed his eyes.

Yeah, sell your crazy to the nurse.

"Nah, they'd get mad."

"They would? Okay. How about you give me the razor so you can't cut yourself even if they want you to?"

"I can't do that either."

"Well, you're better off if you give it to me because they're going to be really mad if the blacksuits have to take it. And you'll lose your TV anyway. If you have the razor, they'll consider you armed and may use the shock shield. I bet the voices would like that even less."

I know. It sounds like I'm saying "just wait until your father gets home." But they'd either come spray him in the face with pepper spray until he handed it over, or they would break out the shock shield—think the polymer shields cops use for crowd control, but electrified—to incapacitate him so he couldn't hurt anyone else, including himself.

"Put out your hand," he commanded.

Oh, hell no. I didn't know where his blood had been. He had long enough arms; he could reach out and cut me if I put my hand out.

"Drop it on the floor and I'll get it."

"You don't trust me?" He sounded hurt.

I almost snorted out loud. I didn't trust anybody. "You *can't* be trusted right now." As if he could ever be. He was an inmate. Now that doesn't mean I thought they were all dog shit, but if the voices really were talking to him, his behavior and reactions were going to be unpredictable. And if he was trying to pull some kind of con, then I had to be especially wary. "Would you trust someone who told you they heard voices? I'm just trying to help you."

The razor clattered to the floor and I picked it up gingerly, careful not to let the edges come in contact with my skin— even though I wore gloves, the razor could easily slice through both the latex and my flesh. I called the OIC over the radio to send another officer to come watch this guy while we called mental health.

As I walked back to the officer's station, an inmate in another cell yelled out my name. I turned to look and a skinny black inmate with long braids motioned for me to come over.

"Not right now, guy. I'll be there in a few minutes after I handle this, okay?"

"It's an emergency!" he demanded. His forehead was sweaty and his eyes were wide and from what I could see of his body, it looked like he was jumping up and down.

What now? I took the stairs two at a time and came to stand in front of his cell. It was definitely not an emergency. He was jacking off.

"Really? Are you kidding me?"

He grinned really big, as if he was proud of himself, and held his cock out with one hand while he continued to stroke with the other. "Nope."

"Well you should be. That little thing is a waste of anyone's time."

I trudged back down to the office. I wasn't embarrassed or horrified that he was naked. I saw upwards of six hundred dicks a day, and one more wasn't a big deal. No, it pissed me off that he interrupted something so urgent to show me his dick. Which looked like every other dick I'd ever seen. Black, white, yellow, brown, blue—it was all still penis.

What was that supposed to do for me? Was I supposed to fall over on my back like some turtle and gasp at the amazing wonder that was his cock? Sorry. Not going to happen. I wasn't impressed.

So then I not only had the ton of paperwork for the mental health guy, but then I had to write a disciplinary report for the dick smacker.

Why did I want to work Seg again?

day 6

HOLY HELL.
I drank way too much, but honestly, I'd needed it after the week I had.

My temples pounded like a bass drum and my eyes didn't want to open. Christ, it was bright.

I thought about rolling over and going back to sleep. I hadn't come in until after four. It was only eight. But today was kid day. I was taking them to the zoo.

One-hundred-degree heat, tired animals in cages licking their own nuts, and bad food. Just like work.

I rolled over and looked at my girls sleeping in the bed next to me. They were so sweet when they were asleep. Their narrow chests rose and fell slowly. The sweet baby curve to their cheeks was smooth in the bright sun. My oldest was nine and she'd lost the toddler chubbiness to her hands. Her fingers were splayed on the pillow and I petted each one softly, wondering what those hands were capable of doing. What she would do with her life, what she would become.

My youngest, her hands were still dimpled and soft. Her bow mouth had fallen open and she sounded like a baby bear; her light snores endeared her to me even more. This one was only a child when she slept. When she was awake, her very old soul was in the driver's seat and she looked on everything with a very adult detachment and disdain. I wondered too what she would mold out of her life.

And I wondered when I'd get my own shit together. They deserved better than living in their grandparents' house with a mom they hardly ever saw. The little one had told me she wanted to go live with her dad because there was more room and she missed him. I said yes and when she asked me if I was upset, I said no. I told her I'd miss her, but it was okay. Then I'd gone to take a shower and I bawled until the hot water ran out.

My oldest's eyes popped open and she still looked like Boo from *Monsters, Inc.* with her large, chocolate doe eyes. "Zoo!" she half-whispered.

I nodded with a grin, even though shaking my head like that made my eyeballs roll around my head and my stomach roiled.

Oh, what the hell? I ran to the bathroom and puked up the cupcakes I'd eaten yesterday in a pungent brew of Hostess and beer. I realized with horror I had a hangover. I'd spent my teen years drinking like a fish, I even drank some in my twenties, but it was like as soon as I hit thirty, someone flipped a switch and it was time to pay up. I'd never had a hangover before.

"You okay, Mommy?"

"We don't have to go to the zoo if you don't feel good. Are you sick?"

No, I'm not sick. I'm just an asshole. I wanted to lie back down and go back to sleep until my head stopped throbbing and my stomach stopped protesting, but I didn't.

"No, babies. Get ready. How about breakfast at the Awful Waffle?"

They shrieked with joy, and I puked again as the sound echoed through my head.

I was sick again at the Awful Waffle, as we had come to call the local all-night waffle place. This time from the other end. It was so loud, I'm sure that the other patrons heard me. I'm sure that people on the interstate heard me.

I didn't know then it would just get worse. I didn't discover until two years later that I had celiac disease. I was allergic to wheat, barley, and oats. So those pitchers of Boulevard Wheat were literally killing me.

I'm sure the waffles didn't help.

I spent more than I meant to after we got to the zoo. I never got to see my kids while I was working the second shift, two in the afternoon to ten at night. They were always asleep by the time I got home. We'd gotten more time because of the summer, but I knew when they went back to school I'd only see them on my days off.

Sometimes, when I think back to this time, I wonder how I ever got through it. How we ever got through it.

The husband and I staggered our days off so it was never an issue of who had them when. He was good about that too. He never ditched them, never forgot, never chose to do anything else than spend time with his kids when it was his turn. He never balked at taking them when it *wasn't* his turn, like when I had to go to the hospital with my mother. No matter what was wrong between us, he tried to be a good father.

And I tried to be a good mother. We ate again at the zoo because they wanted funnel cake, corn dogs, and slushes. We did every little extra thing there was to do: we took the train, rode the carousel, and I bought them everything they looked at longingly with their big anime child eyes in the gift shop. Except for the live crabs. The husband had taken custody of the cat and my parents had a dog. The poor crabs would be harried until either the cat or the dog succeeded in getting to them. All the while, I made discreet stops in the bathrooms after every time I ate.

I swore I'd never drink again.

day 7

I SPENT A LITTLE BIT OF TIME ONLINE TALKING TO FRIENDS who I didn't seem to have a connection with anymore. One friend in particular though, I'll call her Sunshine here, seemed to just accept me and the mess that was my life. She wanted to hear about it and I found myself talking. I didn't open up the floodgates and dump on her, but I told her about the separation. She tried to be encouraging, had a lot of good things to share, but I wasn't ready to hear them yet. Rather than be angry I wasn't ready, she did what good friends do. She let me know she'd be there and she was ready to listen whenever I needed her. I thanked her, but I didn't take her up on it. Not for a long time.

That's part of The Job, as I've said. Isolation. We're supposed to keep the gritty dark away from the outside world. We're supposed to be two people. But it's infinitely easier to be one. So, we tend to slowly sever our connections with people outside our world.

Not with any malice or intent; it just happens.

I had an email from a tower rat friend of mine who wanted me to go to the country bar with him and a few others that night. I hate country music, for the most part. I'm a metal head. But I was lonely and patently unhappy with my life. I thought maybe a little fun would help.

And I vowed I'd only have one beer.

day 8

I DIDN'T KNOW AQUA NET COULD MELT.

Of course, I knew it was flammable. When I was a kid, I used it and my mother's lighter as a mosquito repellent. Flamethrower. Whatever.

I spent summers in Minnesota, and their state bird is the mosquito. Loved visiting my grandma, but at night, when I had the window open and a swarm of them that looked like something out of a Japanese horror movie clung to the screen, I had my doubts about if the screen would keep them out. Or if it did, I was sure their long suckers could squeeze through the little holes in the screen and suck me dry. So I toasted them all. They crackled like Rice Krispies.

On a bastard summer day when I volunteered to get some more experience in Segregation, I suddenly knew what they felt like. The temperature roasted at one hundred degrees outside, and inside, it was twenty degrees hotter. I didn't do much to my hair for work. I put it up in a bun or used a jaw-clip so it was off my collar, but I did curl my bangs. I secured them so even a tornado wouldn't ruffle my appearance.

That took a lot of Aqua Net.

Which promptly melted from my bangs and slid down into my eyes.

My eyes started burning worse than when we'd had to get

sprayed with CS gas and take a shot of pepper spray to the face in training. Tears are your eyes' self-defense mechanism, so they just started pouring down my cheeks.

It looked for all the world like I was bawling.

"What's wrong, Sarge? Somebody hurt your feelings?"

"Look at the girl crying on the tier," another inmate hooted.

"Shut the fuck up. I got hair spray melting in my eye," I growled.

"Sure you do. We understand. Even a hardass like you has to take a day off." Laughing ensued.

"Hey, don't rile her up. It's too hot for this shit."

"No shit. Why don't you guys grieve this?" I asked them, referring to their complaint process. They would grieve anything as "cruel and unusual," up to and including their incarceration if the state would let them. I'd say slowly baking to death in high summer in this kind of heat was cruel and unusual. Not just for them, but for me too. The prison was more than a hundred years old. It was made out of brick. Summer time turned it into a big oven.

I'd seen an inmate grieve standard operating procedure that's there for his safety—and win. But I'd seen reasonable grievances fail. Like one inmate who was allergic to fish and soy. All he got every single day, every meal, was peanut butter and lettuce. That's not a reasonable diet, which he is entitled to, but he lost. Or the practicing Satanist denied his right to freedom of religion. The prison pastor argued it was a hate group and not a real religion. No matter that most of the religious groups in prison are fronts for sex, dealing and trading, gang activity...this guy only wanted to be free to have a Baphomet icon in his cell. He wasn't asking to hold a religious callout or any special treatment. He just wanted to be able to order religious paraphernalia like any other group.

But this rejection was from the same bastard who refused to show Harry Potter on the prison TV channel, not because it might incite the pedophiles but because he deemed it anti-Christian. Hey, where's the separation of church and state? Not seeing it here. If I was an inmate, you can bet I'd grieve the violation of my religious freedom. You lose a lot of rights when you go to prison, but your freedom of religion isn't supposed to be one of them.

Further, where was the damn air-conditioning?

Heat makes people angry. It's a proven fact crimes of passion go up in the summer time. Yeah, so let's throw three hundred criminals together in an enclosed place and turn up the heat. That's bright.

"If anyone wants a grievance, I'll be passing them out with chow."

In Seg, we had to pass chow around since they didn't get to come out to eat. Not only did I have Aqua Net in my eye, I was also sweating like a hog. I don't mean a little sweaty, I mean it poured off me like I just got out of a pool. Only it wasn't chlorinated water, it was body filth. I was embarrassed by it, and I even felt sorry that I served their food.

Of course a few commented on it. How they wouldn't eat anything from a fat, sweaty hog like me, and I had to agree. I wouldn't either. I could have written them up, but it was the truth. Skinny, fat, average, it didn't matter. It was gross no matter who did it.

The end of the day in Seg was the worst, after chow had been passed, trays had been collected, and showers had been completed. Inmates weren't allowed out of their cells to dump their trash, so they just threw it out on the run and the inmate workers had to clean it up.

In the summer, the prison always stank, but Seg in the summer was especially horrible. It stank like bad breath, body funk, and rotten garbage with a hint of MSG from the ramen they made in their cells. The guys were only mandated to wash once a week, so there was the regular dirty body stench plus whatever they had fermenting. The guy who pissed all over his cell? That wasn't especially out of the ordinary. Some would empty out toothpaste tubes and keep their feces in it for special times when they needed a shit gun. Those were especially effective. Or they'd try to hoard leftovers from meals and it would spoil. Some used their toilets like refrigerators, putting their containers of milk down in the water in hopes it would keep it cool. And some were just dirty and didn't want to wash.

When we finished that night, I was ready to go home. Completely exhausted. I felt like I'd done a good job, that the OIC would see I was an asset.

But one of my friends had called during shift. His wife had left him. She didn't even do him the courtesy of telling him she was going. She just took the car, leaving him stranded at work, and drove a few hundred miles to her mother's. She'd also taken their daughter with no explanation and no mention of when he could see her.

He said he was happy to see the bitch go, but fuck her if she was going to take his kid away.

And he said he really needed a drink.

So I went.

Don't get me wrong, I'm not blaming him. I chose to go. If I just wanted to be supportive, I could have gone with him and stuck to my decision not to drink myself into oblivion. I chose to go, I chose to drink, and I chose not to stop after I'd obviously had enough.

But at least I didn't lie to myself in the morning and say I wasn't going to do it again.

day 9

I DIDN'T HAVE A HANGOVER, BUT I WAS DAMN TIRED THE next day.

I was in a tower, which a lot of people would have enjoyed, but not me. I hated the tower. It was boring and when you're tired, that makes it all too easy to fall asleep.

Well, I hated the tower except for the fact it was air-conditioned. I had that thing set so low I could've hung a side of beef in there.

Because working the tower bored most people, there were stories galore of tower mishaps. From some dumbass playing Wild Bill with his shotgun "It misfired on its own, I swear!" and shooting down into the Captain's office to yet another Darwin Award Nominee dropping her weapon onto the yard and then dropping a bucket after it and asking an inmate to pick the weapon up so she could haul it back up—it was just a disaster waiting to happen. Yes, let's hand a loaded M14 to a violent felon. Go on. Great idea.

I'm not stupid, so I didn't think anything *that* terrible would happen, but I do have a klutz gene. If there is a pothole to trip over, I'll find it. So I despised the tower, although I've always enjoyed the sound a 12-gauge makes when you rack it. It's also fun to do it with the loudspeaker on and watch everyone on the yard hit the deck, but the powers that be frowned on that, considered it an unnecessary use of force.

It was a fairly uneventful shift. I spent a good portion of it on the phone to the other towers. Had to do something to stay awake, and I was still observing my area, etc., and so forth.

Until it was time for trash. The big dumpster was within my area of control, and I was responsible for running the gates that would allow the inmate workers in and out of the space.

One of the guys on the crew was one I'd known for some time. He was tall, a huge beast of a guy, really. He was white but spent most of his time with the Bloods. He talked to me every day. Always had a "hello" and a joke. That was part of our repartee. You get to know certain guys, but there's a fine line. Never anything personal or anything that could be considered on a deeper level than interactions you have with any other inmate.

This makes it hard because there are always people who click more easily than others. There will be people you like and people you don't. But you have to treat them all the same.

I knew a lot of people who had trouble with this guy. He was a known troublemaker. Shit-stirrer, they called him. I didn't doubt it, but I never had that sort of interaction with him.

He called out to signal he needed to go past the gate, and I came outside onto the walk (a small sidewalk area like an observation deck outside the tower) with my M14 shouldered, as was appropriate.

"Look at you with your gun." He said this as if it were something cute I'd done—a little girl wearing her mother's heels. But I wasn't a little girl and I wasn't wearing heels. I was wearing an M14.

Here we go. He stood there with the rest of the street crew—other inmates who took care of small maintenance issues, etc. He was fronting for his boys.

"Yep," I said, and just nodded.

The officer with him raised a brow at the exchange, but I ignored him. I had to make my own reputation. If I'd allowed the other officer to handle it for me, or if I'd deferred to him, my rep would be in the crapper.

"You wouldn't shoot me," he said with a big grin.

Yeah, actually I would. Part of my interview when I applied for the job consisted of:

Interviewer: Could you shoot someone if you had to?
Me: Yes.
Interviewer: You're hired.

And I would. The Seg OIC who'd been in 'Nam said that it was easy to say I would pull the trigger, but actually doing it was something else entirely. I respect what he tried to say with that statement, but I know me and I know if it was me or the inmate, I'd shoot him with no hesitation, and I wouldn't feel bad about it.

When I tried therapy for another issue, the therapist told me this was a sign of sociopathy if I could really do that. She said it like it was the most horrible thing in the world that I would kill a person. But I didn't see it as killing a person. I saw it as neutralizing a threat. Keeping the dark things in cages and behind walls. That's what I was paid to do.

I guess her diagnosis should have bothered me, but it didn't. A psychiatrist I worked with as a secretary, not a patient, once told me that most law enforcement and Special Forces types have similar brain function to serial killers and exhibit antisocial and sociopathic tendencies. It all depends on how it's used, whether for the betterment of society and within acceptable confines or without.

It's something that if we don't have when we start the job, we have to cultivate it to be effective. We have to separate ourselves from them, and it's for their own good as well as ours. So we treat them all the same, no matter what horrible crime they've committed. We have to inure ourselves to the horror of a father who would rape his Down syndrome daughter and father a child with her. The horror of a man who drove around in his car with his dead wife in the trunk for a month, eating pieces of her body. Looking into the eyes of a killer and knowing what's looking back at you isn't quite human. A predator higher up on the food chain. Faster, smarter, stronger, and waiting to pounce.

So could I shoot him?

What about if I couldn't? That was the more important question because the ramifications of my answer had a much broader reach. What if he climbed the wall and I couldn't pull that trigger? I'd be responsible for every atrocity he committed. Would I rather his blood be on my hands or the blood of a child he raped and dismembered? The mother he guts, the cop he shoots and kills while he's in pursuit?

He said it again. "I talk to you every day, girly. Quit acting like you'd be able to pull that trigger."

I don't need to talk shit. I know what I would do and what I wouldn't. That's part of our training too. Examine every situation and plan for every eventuality. Go over it in our heads. I still do that in every place I go. I always spot the exits and try to plan for every contingency.

"Climb the wall and see." I shrugged with a grin.

That was enough. It told him our interaction didn't have to change, but it also told him where I stood. His crew too.

"Aww, it's like that? You're a hard woman." He joked and put on a smile, but we understood each other.

Yeah, it was exactly like that.

Something I almost had to prove the next day.

day 10

HOSPITAL DUTY.

I'd never done it before, but I'd heard that hospital duty was even more boring than tower duty. I didn't think that was possible.

I told the officer I relieved I'd never done it before, and he said it was no big deal. Just make sure the inmate doesn't leave the room, don't let him have calls or visitors, keep him cuffed to the railing of the bed unless he needs to use the john, and if he does, make him leave the door open.

Seems simple enough, right?

Wrong.

Inmate was a talker. As soon as he opened his suck, it didn't close. I probably could have landed a 747 inside his jaw and he'd have been talking around it. Big jaw—he had a large frame. I could tell by the way his feet hung off the end of the bed that he was taller than me. He was tatted all up his arms with a shaved head, and he had a distinct tweaker look about him. He could have been a big guy if he'd gotten off whatever shit he was on.

He was also missing half his calf muscle. Of course, I had to hear about how that happened too. Cancer. But of course it was the state's fault because the cops Tasered him when they took him down after a seventy-two-hour standoff in which he'd killed four police officers and his wife.

Then he whined for me to take off his cuffs. The cuffs were hurting his ankle.

Yeah, right after he tells me he's a filthy cop killer, he wants some sympathy? He wouldn't have gotten any anyway, but that's not a bright move. But I could tell he didn't consider me a cop. To him, I was a rent-a-pig or a cage kicker. We're not good enough to be cops.

I wouldn't uncuff him, so he hit his call button for the nurse.

"You know, with his leg like that, he's not going any-where," the nurse said, eyeing me disdainfully. "You can take the cuffs off."

Like bloody hell I would.

"Sorry. Can't do it."

"It's inhumane," she growled.

"Tell that to the families of the people he killed, honey."

She snorted and rolled her eyes and left.

Yeah, cry me a river of purple panther piss. Sure, they're still people and should be treated as such, but not to the point of endangering others. What's next? Prison is too hard, so it's in-humane to send them there? Slippery slope.

Then he said he had to go to the bathroom. So I unlocked the cuffs, knowing it was going to be a huge hassle to get him back in them, but I couldn't deny him the bathroom. At least, not at this juncture.

I reiterated he should leave the door open, and as I did, a different nurse came back in with his lunch tray. I crossed away from my chair to the other side of the room to get out of her way, and as soon as he came out and a look crossed his face, I knew I'd fucked up. I just wasn't sure how.

He bent over my chair and pulled out a big black bag, out of which he produced a bottle of state-issued pepper spray.

Apparently, the officer I relieved of duty and the Control officer who'd sent me on duty had both neglected to inform me about a duty bag and that it held such goodies as a belly chain for transport back to the prison, extra restraints, and pepper spray to force compliance in case of an attempted assault or escape.

He had it aimed at me with a cold smile, eyes dead and flat. "What do we have here?"

The nurse had flattened herself against the wall, afraid to move.

What did we have here? My dick in a sling if I didn't get that spray back from him. I really didn't want to take another shot of pepper spray in the face, but I didn't want him to escape or take the nurse hostage. Or do any number of horrible things that could have happened.

He had pepper spray, but I had a .38. Not my favorite—I hated the .38, vastly preferring the 12-gauge. But I'd make do with what I had.

"Put it down," I commanded in the most even, calm tone I could manage.

"No, I don't think I will." He grinned wider and tossed the canister back and forth between his hands.

Yeah, so I might take a shot of pepper spray in the face. Whatever. I had before. It would sting like a motherfucker, but I had six bullets to neutralize the threat. Even with my eyes on fire, I could still hit center mass. He was a big target.

I took a breath. My hands weren't even shaking. I drew my gun with no hesitation. "I'm going to tell you one more time to put the spray down." Hopefully it would drive home the fact that I *would* shoot him.

I didn't want to.

But I would.

Lives depended on my choices.

Given his history, I already knew part of what he was capable of, and that would be on me if I let him escape.

In a split second I imagined the scenario, pulling the trigger, the aftermath. The face of his daughter and if I could look at her after.

Could I? If I wounded him? If I killed him?

Yes, I could.

"Put the pepper spray down on the table and back away slowly. This is your last chance to comply," I said firmly.

"Or what? You'll shoot me?" He took a step toward me.

I inhaled deeply.

And I'd fire on the exhale.

Cool and smooth. On target. Center mass.

He dropped it and held his hands high. "It's not like I could do anything. I'm missing half my leg."

He didn't need his leg to kill the nurse. Or the cops who would have pursued him. Especially not since he was a tweaker. If he'd been high, a bullet might not have stopped him. Maybe not even all six.

"Close your mouth, and sit on the bed."

He did as I ordered, and I recuffed him after holstering my weapon. I put him in the belly chain too, restrained him so he couldn't go for my gun. The nurse suggested they catheterize him so he didn't need to leave the bed. I told her as medical staff, that was her call.

When I recuffed his ankle in addition to his wrist, I saw a red circle starting to chafe where the cuff had been, where the skin was obviously thin and about to break open.

I wrapped a washcloth around his ankle to build a barrier

between the metal and his flesh. Not so much he could even shift the cuff around, but enough so that it didn't tear his skin open.

One might ask why I'd give a fuck after what had just happened, but like I said, it was my job.

day 11

"Hey, Lunsford. How's it hangin'?" one of the yard workers called to me as I walked into the enclosure for the first rec period of the shift.

I was a yard dog that night, which meant it would be me and two or three other officers walking around while three hundred inmates had their rec time. This was a dangerous post because when things kicked off (be it a riot, fight, shanking, etc.), it was usually on the yard or in the chow hall. In fact, it had only been a few years since an officer had been beaten to death with free weights on the yard.

"A little to the left," I answered.

He laughed. "Aw, I know that's right. You're OG, Lunsford. O. G." He accentuated both letters individually.

"Back at you." I nodded my head in acknowledgment.

OG means original gangster. He had told me before I was "old school," both terms that most inmates and uniformed staff respected because someone who's OG got things done. No touchy-feely let's-talk-about-our-feelings bullshit that nonuniformed staff who don't deal with the inmates on a day-to-day basis think is a good idea. You and the inmates both do what you have to do. More often than not it puts you at odds with each other, but there's a certain amount of respect there too. On both sides. The inmate tries to get something past you and you try to make sure that doesn't happen, and you both understand it's just part of the game.

The best part? The lines are clear. There is no miscommunication about what's expected from either party.

It's the difference between convict and inmate, and officer and guard. And yeah, there is most definitely a difference. Convicts do their time with their heads down. They don't bitch and they don't snitch. There's a saying in prison: Snitches get stitches. But convicts are a rare and dying breed. Prison culture has become popular in the mainstream, glorified in media, and these men who come to prison now behave like inmates. Those that I'd call convict rather than inmate are few and far between.

An officer does his job and gives them what they have coming and nothing else. Officers are fair, firm, and consistent. Officers are professionals who do their jobs and put their lives on the line every day. We're officers the same as any other law enforcement and enforce state and federal laws within the scope of our duties. A guard is sloppy, lazy, inconsistent, illiterate, easily bought—a finger-up-the-nose-to-the-first-knuckle waste of space. To call us guards is an insult that's damn near in the "fighting words" category.

This convict went about the business of readying the equipment for use, and I went about finishing my prep too. I had a pre-rec check of the yard to complete. Checking for holes in fencing, modified equipment, contraband, etc.

"That's an interesting rapport you have with him," a man said from outside the fencing as I began my checks.

I shrugged halfheartedly. In corrections, that shrug translated to "it is what it is." A common phrase used universally throughout law enforcement.

"Can I come in?" he asked.

I looked at him again, assessing him. He was as tall as I was, and I was about six-foot-one in my boots, wearing khakis and a white polo. He had dark hair, cropped closely to his head, and wore the type of no-nonsense black framed glasses that are often called "rape prevention goggles." Very cheap, also very easy to replace. He wore tennis shoes, not the boots that officers wore.

"Can I see your ID?" I had no idea who this guy was and when in doubt, always ID. He could have been a visitor who'd wandered off, someone sent to test me to see if I would challenge him for his ID, or he could have been an inmate who was trying to get into one particular yard/rec time or another—one where he wasn't supposed to be. He could have even stolen those clothes from somewhere and this could be part of an escape.

He flashed his ID. The Unit Team Manager for Segregation. This was the oh-my-God interview. Son of a bitch. And here he'd caught me without my company face on. Well, nothing to it but to do it, right? I let him in and he walked with me as I completed my checks.

"Yeah, well, you know we're all individuals and what works with some people doesn't work for others. You have to communicate in a language they understand."

"Very interesting. Tell me more," he said as we continued around the yard.

God, I can't believe how thick the crap was that was coming out of my mouth…I'm good at that, affecting my behavior to blend in with those around me. Although working at the prison made me less inclined to bother with any filter for anyone and effectively killed any tolerance I had for bullshit. And that's what it was, changing my mode of speech to suit someone else's sensibilities. Bullshit. Yet, as I spewed what I knew he wanted to hear, I knew some of it was true.

I debated the next example and decided to go ahead and tell him. "For instance, when I first worked in D cell house out on OJT (on the job training), I asked an inmate to please go to his cell, and he laughed at me. He said, 'Look at this bitch here with her pretty manners. Don't you know you're in prison, girl?' I smiled and asked him if he'd rather I said, 'Lock the fuck up, you shit-bag motherfucker.' He stopped for a minute and really did take time to consider, and he decided he'd rather I said please and treated him like a man. I told him I would be happy to treat him with respect and courtesy as long as he did the same."

"You know you're not supposed to use that kind of language. He could have written you up." The unit team manager looked at me disapprovingly.

"Yes, I know." I nodded. "But I could have written him up for failing to follow a direct order and sent him to Seg. It comes down to communication. Some of these guys grew up in an environment where courtesy and respect are seen as weakness, and they don't understand what you're saying to them unless there are a few 'fucks' sprinkled throughout. It doesn't get their attention otherwise because it's not their native language. It's also thinking outside the box. There could have been paper on both sides, but there wasn't, and I haven't had any issue with that inmate since the interaction. I think it was a great opportunity for risk reduction."

He seemed to chew this over for some time. He asked me more questions, but I knew even though he may not have liked my methods that I'd said the right words. *Risk reduction.* That's what everyone was about, and it looked really good on paper.

Then he told me that the OIC had already told him that he

wanted me for the post. He said he still had a few more people to interview, but as it stood, he wanted me for the post too. It was vital that they both wanted me. The OIC, a first sergeant, was in charge of everything security related in the cell house, but the Unit Team Manager was responsible for all administrative matters.

I was elated. Something was going right.

Until later that night after shift when I was standing out in the parking lot across the street from the prison, where we'd gather to bitch and complain, generally letting off steam before going home.

My engine overheated, and my piece-of-shit Camry burst into flame.

day 12

THE NEXT DAY THE FRIEND WHO WAS SUPPOSED TO PICK me up for work forgot, and I didn't have enough money to call a cab or any minutes on my cell phone. So I had to hoof it about a mile up the street to the nearest pay phone. I had fifty cents to my name. Enough to make *one* phone call.

I called my husband so he could come and get me when he got off his shift at the prison, and so he could also call the Captain and tell him I was going to be late and why. I wasn't worried about how that would affect my career because I was usually a consistent employee and accepted overtime shifts and extra responsibilities.

It turned out to be another tower day and halfway through the shift, my oldest daughter called. She was elated. She'd started her period.

We talked about it; I asked her if she had any questions. I made a big deal about it being a good and positive thing. Told her I'd buy her something special to celebrate and we'd have a grown-up dinner out together. When we hung up, I cried like a little bitch.

I was missing so much of her life working this second shift (2–10) and living as we were. I didn't see any other avenue for us though. That made it worse. I felt trapped in this mess I'd made trying to get out of the *other* mess I'd made of my life. It was a vicious circle.

But I plugged it up. It was prison. I was behind the walls, and my personal bullshit had no place there. Even hanging out by myself up in the tower, as it were.

day 13

THE HUSBAND TOOK ME TO LUNCH SO WE COULD TALK about the kids, but invariably, the conversation turned to The Job. When we were together, no subject had ever been taboo, and with both of us working there, it was the natural progression of the conversation.

Tensions, rumors, his snitches, my snitches, and just what was going on in general. More caches of shanks had been found. Some in cells, some on the yard. Guys were hoarding newspapers and magazines they weren't supposed to have, and, in most cases, they'd use it for armor. Numbers were up in Seg, with inmates doing stupid shit to get in there. Inmates who were normally no problem were walking up to officers out of the blue and threatening to shank them. Why? It's a check-in move designed to take them out of population and into protective custody but without looking like a pussy or spilling whatever information they have.

Some of the brass would have frowned on us and this conversation. Talking about all of this stuff outside of work was in effect "taking it home." In training, they tell us not to take it home. That's universal throughout corrections. My father was a federal corrections officer, and he never brought it home. He never told me anything about what happened at work beyond what I absolutely had to know, until I did The Job myself.

As a kid, there was almost a whole year in which I didn't see my father. He worked eighteen-hour days with no time off, for months at a time, during what came to be called the Cuban Crisis. I don't remember details, only that inmates were lighting their mattresses on fire and there were riots. They had to go on lockdown.

Shortly after this, or at least shortly to my kid memory, an officer was killed. Not on The Job, though, but at home. He brought The Job home with him, they said, and he took it out on his family. He'd beat his wife almost to death. I remember overhearing my mother and the other wives talking about the night he chased her with a baseball bat and she was crying and pounding on doors to see if someone would let her in.

His son had finally had enough and killed him with his own gun.

It was one of the times I asked my dad about his job because I saw him on television behind yellow crime scene tape. Looking back on it now, it was like that scene from *The Godfather* where Al Pacino tells Diane Keaton not to ask him about his business. He told me he couldn't and wouldn't talk about it, that I didn't need to know those things.

There were many nights my father would come home and just sit silently in his chair. Sometimes, I don't know how he did it. He didn't go out with friends, he didn't drink, and he didn't do anything but work and come home. He did woodworking in his spare time, but that wasn't really a hobby. It was like a second job. A little country-themed craft store in town sold his work and took orders for commissioned projects to help put food on the table.

He had a good reputation as an honest man, but he was a hard-ass too.

During my first stint working at the prison, the prison dentist picked me up in a bar. He'd worked both at the federal level and at the state. We were on our way back to his house and conversation turned to The Job, and when he found out who my dad was, he apologized profusely and asked me not to tell my dad that I'd met him and especially not that he'd tried to take me home.

When I was a teenager and still in my rebellious fuck-you-all stage, I used to like to bring home the most inappropriate guys, but there was one line I wouldn't cross. He couldn't have done time. If he had, my father would have buried me in a shallow grave with lime in the crawl space. He pretty much kept his opinions about other guys to himself; he'd just give them that thousand-yard stare. By the time I was seventeen, he stopped bothering to learn their names.

Until the guy I met at the biker bar.

Everyone knew me down there and they'd serve me and my friends. My friend's dad had taken us in there and bought us beers and smokes, so after that, they served us every time. We knew to put the beers down if they got raided and to say we were only there for the karaoke.

This guy, he was all that a rebellious little antisocial like me could want. He had twenty tattoos, long hair, a Harley, a jaw like a brick, and his biceps were bigger than my head. He was also about six-foot-three. He read poetry and quoted Byron and Keats to me while we were dancing. He even got into a bar fight over my honor. Some guy had called me a slut and asked how much I'd cost him. This guy had been big too, as big as my biker. With just as many tattoos. He had more patches on his jacket though. Which I learned later meant he was higher up in his gang. But he got his ass handed to him in two pieces, and he was banned from the bar. My biker couldn't have been any more perfect if his name had been Snot.

He came to pick me up and my dad answered the door. By now, my dad had gotten used to the company I kept and knew the less he said, the more likely I'd get tired of them and they'd go away. But this one was different. I knew it as soon as my dad opened the door and the guy's posture changed. His eyes narrowed and the badass biker started sniveling like a little bitch.

"Lieutenant. *SIR*."

I didn't even have to see my father's face. I knew then he'd done federal time. I didn't say a damn word. In fact, I don't think I could have gotten to my room faster if my ass had been on fire. I sat on my bed, waiting for my father to come in and talk to me/murder me slowly. But nothing happened. We never spoke of it again.

I called the guy the next day and the first thing he said was, "You didn't tell me who your dad was." Like it was somehow my fault.

"You didn't tell me you'd done time," I shrieked.

"That's not something I usually talk about on a first date."

"Why the hell not? You know this is a prison town." We had the federal prison, state prison, community corrections, CCA (Corrections Corporation of America, a privately run corrections facility), county jail, military detention barracks—we were loaded to the brim with prison.

"I didn't think you were *that* Sasek's daughter."

"Yeah, because we all know Sasek is like Smith. Really? Are you kidding me? I'm lucky I'm not dead."

"You? I was the one there to pick up his precious and only daughter."

"I thought you were a badass. You're sniveling."

"I'm not ashamed to admit your father terrifies me. He could ruin my parole."

"And you're on parole? Oh. My. God." My dad could have gotten in serious trouble at work for that since this guy was still on paper, as we called it, meaning he still had an active file.

"I don't think we should see each other."

"Well, no shit."

"He's not mad, is he?"

I hung up without answering him.

But that wasn't taking The Job home; that was The Job coming to him.

I looked at my husband over lunch as I remembered this, and I tried to imagine what he'd do if one of our girls brought home someone he knew from his cell house. I imagine his reaction would be much the same. My husband and my father don't like each other very much, and it makes me laugh because in a lot of ways, they're a lot alike. It wasn't always this way, but now as I'm writing this and my husband has done The Job for a few years and he's good at it, the similarities are ridiculous.

Except my husband does bring it home, but not in a bad way. Meaning it's not heavy or subversive. He brings it home, we talk about it. Part of it could be because I've been there, I've done it. I know the places he's talking about, I know the policies, I know the frustrations and the little victories. There shouldn't be anything we can't share; making an officer be two people drives a wedge into any relationship: platonic, familial, or romantic.

When we both were working there, it was common ground when everything else seemed so far apart.

Like this day. We talked. We laughed. We commiserated. We ate french fries. And it was good. Even when our conversation turned to the darker parts of The Job, not just commiserating over the same stressors and pressures but the horror of which only humanity is capable of.

Like when he told me about the inmate who tried to disembowel himself with the jagged lid of a tuna can.

That takes a certain kind of horrible dedication to carve at yourself and pull out your own guts. He was a sex offender, a diaper sniper (child molester). He was also Latino. That's something that the Latin gangs won't tolerate. The population at the prison where I worked was different than most because we had the only sex offender treatment program in the state, so these offenders weren't victimized as often as sex offenders are in other populations simply because we had so many. But the Latin gangs don't care. One of their own? They'd torment him until they killed him or he killed himself.

This inmate had tried to kill himself seven times. The staff would save his life, and then as soon as he was back in general population the gang members would take after him with a lock in a sock, gang rape, and anything else they could think of to torment him.

This time he slit his wrists too, and he bled out before he could get emergency care.

You're probably wondering how I felt about hearing this. It's an awful way to die, to be so tormented that you'd pull out your own intestines. If I was the officer on duty, I would have done my job to get him emergency care. I would have followed protocol. But his death wouldn't and didn't keep me up at night.

It's a wretched state of affairs when the only commonality you have with someone you love is another person's death and pain. But sometimes, that's just the life working The Job.

day 14

I PUT A DEPOSIT DOWN ON AN APARTMENT. I NEEDED MY own space. It was a little box of a place, but I didn't care. It was mine.

And I got news about the car. I could fix it, but it would take all of my furniture money. If it wasn't one thing, it was another.

But I didn't let that stop me. I had to have my own place. I don't do well living under someone else's rules, and I don't do well with sick people either. I don't know how I'm supposed to act. So rather than subject myself to that discomfort, I avoid it.

One would think since I didn't like living under someone else's rules, that I'd have more sympathy for the inmates. But I hadn't fucked up and gone to prison, so I was free to live by my own rules, within reason—as they would be if they hadn't gone to prison.

I had a place to live but no furniture, and I couldn't really afford to rent any. Not with how much I was drinking, and I wasn't ready to give up going out with friends for nice furniture. But there was too much going on to really worry about it. There were plenty of people who had it worse. Or who made it worse for themselves.

One of my Seg friends called me at home to tell me about what happened to Front Butt.

Front Butt was a guard. He didn't even try to be an officer.

We called him Front Butt because he was so overweight, it looked like his butt was in the front, and he'd earned our derision by being worthless. All he did on shift was eat. He didn't search cells, make checks, or generally do anything but sit on his butt and stuff his face. Not always even with *his own food*. He'd eat anyone's food. He'd take the inmates' food, not items from the chow hall but items from the canteen that inmates had paid for themselves.

The inmates had absolutely no respect for him, and he is a cautionary tale for why it's never safe to eat food you've left unattended. He's lucky he's only a cautionary tale and not a name on a plaque of officers who died in service. Inmates will kill over their food just like any other animal in the wild.

Front Butt was working a dorm in the Medium. They called the floor plan an "honor dorm" because everything was open with no cells and even a microwave for general use.

It had long been known among the inmates that if they left their own food unattended for more than a minute in the microwave when he was working, it would disappear. So they made a special burrito just for him. They opened a soft tortilla and used it like a cracker in a circle jerk—filled it with semen. Then they added some cheese and some canned meat.

He did as predicted and stole the burrito out of the microwave and ate it. All of it.

Then later that night when he was doing count, random inmates asked him how he liked his burrito, and they all started laughing. He didn't recognize any of their voices because he never got out in the dorm and did checks, never had the initiative to identify names with voices and faces.

The story spread through the prison like wildfire, and by the time shift was over, every officer in the prison knew what had happened to Front Butt and the burrito.

He is a prime example of why those of us who dedicate ourselves to The Job despise guards like him. I already mentioned he's lucky they didn't kill him, but if they'd taken any other measures besides what they did, that would have put good officers in jeopardy. There would have been an alarm, with responders and fights—it could have escalated into a riot that could have put even more people in danger. All because one guy couldn't do his job.

There are those who don't belong, and that's why we push them out, cull them from the herd.

It's not cruelty; it's survival.

day 20

SUNSHINE CALLED TO TELL ME SHE WAS GETTING MARRIED.
Joy welled up in me for her. Her mate sounded like an amazing man who was totally and completely in love with everything about her. She'd started a new job she loved and they'd just had a baby. The way she spoke, her life seemed picture perfect—amazing. Not only the specifics, but the generalities too. She'd decided to be happy and she made me wish it was that easy.

Sunshine told me it simply *was* that easy, but we didn't talk about that long. She invited me to the wedding. I was elated.

After we hung up, I remembered how I felt when my husband and I decided to get married, and it made me laugh a little bit, but it was a laugh that was almost crying because it was a badge for what our whole marriage had been. My eyes watered, but I refused to let the tears fall.

My husband proposed to me after a heated argument. With us, everything had included arguing.

We'd fought viciously and I'd kicked him out of the apartment. He'd moved all of his stuff to a friend's house except for his TV. When he came back for the TV, he said it was a shame we were splitting up because he'd had plans for me. Forever plans. I said I had too. He said it wasn't too late and we could still have forever because he didn't want to go. I told him I didn't want him to go. Then he asked me to give him forever.

So much for forever.

I hoped it would be different for Sunshine than it had been for me.

day 23

I WAS WORKING VISITING. I'D BEEN TOLD THAT THE FIRST Sergeant specifically asked for me. That meant he'd try to get me to take the open post in Visiting. It was a specialty post like Segregation, with the same flaming hoops to jump through to get assigned there.

But I wanted Segregation. I didn't want Visiting. I hated it.

I didn't much care for the First Sergeant either.

The prison had gone nonsmoking. No one, not staff, inmates, or visitors, could smoke on prison property. Tobacco became contraband, so being caught with it was the same as being caught with any other substance. It all carried the same charge should the facility decide to prosecute: introducing contraband.

But this guy thought he was a special snowflake. He bragged that he got a note from his doctor that said he had to smoke to relieve stress or it would be dangerous for his heart. He'd already had one heart attack and he acted like the whole world came and went at the leisure of his cardiac health.

Officers had heart attacks all the time. In fact, there was one we called Heart Attack Smith because he'd had four while actually at work and six or seven during the course of his employment. No one was babying him or holding his hand. He still got up and came to work with no expectation of special treatment.

Something about the Visiting OIC always struck me as slimy.

I didn't want to work anywhere near him. I have something my friends and I had come to call a Dirty Bitch Detector. Staff who have been turned by inmates—who bring things in for them or who engage in inappropriate relationships with them—are called dirty bitches, and it seemed I developed an extra sense about those people. I haven't been wrong yet. The OIC didn't quite set off my Dirty Bitch Detector, but he made it twitch.

First off, he was crap about enforcing the rules. If a visitor got too upset about anything, he would always cave, as if he thought Visiting was the prison's customer service department. They aren't customers. They can't take their business elsewhere. When I told him my thoughts, he said that was exactly it. To treat them like customers.

What?

Yet another reason why Visiting was not the right slot for me.

I understand treating the visitors with respect. Of course, they're human beings. I can only imagine how hard it would be to have to come and see your loved one behind bars. To see all of their freedoms taken away and know that there was no chance any of that was going to change in the near future. No matter what their crime, that person is still someone's family. Sure, I get that.

It's all too easy to forget too. That both officers and inmates were someone's child. Someone's father, someone's brother... someone's whole reason for breathing.

But that doesn't mean the rules don't apply to them.

There was a strict dress code for visitors and guidelines for what things they can have on their person when entering the Visiting area. Everyone always had a reason why the rules were for everyone else but them. I have no patience with that kind of behavior.

But there were others who were more than happy to operate within the rules set down as long as that meant they got to see their loved ones.

One inmate's mother, a frail little old woman of about ninety, asked me if I ever worked inside the walls. When I told her I had, she asked me if I knew her son and if he was behaving. I knew her son and it amazed me that he could have sprung from her loins. She was this delicate, bitty creature and he was huge, like a grizzly bear, six-foot-eight with biceps bigger than my head. She told me if he didn't behave or acted disrespectfully toward any of the officers to call her and she'd straighten him out.

That would have been against policy, and I never would have followed through on that threat, but the next time that inmate gave me grief I threatened to tell his mother. The look of horror that bloomed on his face was priceless. He was more afraid of that than a write-up, Seg time, or anything else I could possibly entertain.

day 24

SOMEONE HATED ME.

   Or really liked me. It was torturous either way.

I was stuck in Visiting again.

My face hurt from all the fake smiling I'd had to do. Even my teeth ached.

One of the other Visiting officers came back to Max Visiting from the Minimum, and any time a staff member or visitor leaves the facility, even just to go out to their car, they have to be searched again in order to reenter. I despised working the entry point because this seemed like I was treating staff like inmates. It felt dirty to me. Wrong. But I did it anyway because it was my job.

The other officer wandered through the metal detector and it beeped, but she didn't stop.

"Hey, I need you to empty out your pockets and go through again." I assumed that she'd just forgotten to take her keys out of her pocket or a pen, or some other minutia that would have set off the detector.

Until she said, "Excuse me? Are you serious?" Her nose wrinkled up and twitched like a rabbit's.

No, I'm talking for my health. "Yes, I'm serious. The detector beeped, indicating you have metal somewhere on your person. Put it in the bowl and go through again." I shouldn't have had to explain that to her. In fact, it never should have been an issue. Yeah, it was a hassle, but it was also state law.

"You're fucking serious?"

"I just said as much. Go back through the detector or leave the premises. Your choice."

"I'm calling the boss."

"That's fine. Call him. And I'll call the Lieutenant. Or Captain. I'll tell them that neither you nor the OIC want to follow procedure and be searched."

She walked over to the door into the facility, waiting for me to push the button to buzz her in. I refused.

"Fucking bitch."

"Cunt," I replied in a cheerful tone.

"I'm going to get you fired," she said.

"For what? Calling you a cunt? Do you feel harassed? I don't give a shit. This all comes back down to the part where you don't want to be searched. I'm not the one who's going to be fired."

She still didn't move, and just as I was dialing the Captain's office, the First Sergeant came out. He held the door open for her.

I shook my head. "Don't do that. She set off the metal detector and refused to empty her pockets and go back through."

"Oh, it's fine," he said.

The hell it was. She obviously had something she was trying to take in to the institution that didn't belong. Something that could hurt someone I cared about or me. So when the Captain answered, I told him what had happened. I even included the part where I called her a cunt.

The Captain called the First Sergeant on the radio and demanded he not enter the institution with the officer and came over personally to observe the search. The detector didn't beep the second time around. I'm sure that she had something in her pocket that she passed off somehow.

There were rumors after I left my employment with the state that she was dirty, that she'd been caught inmate fucking, but I never found out for sure one way or another.

But that had never been a boat I wanted to sail on, and after that, they didn't want me back in Visiting.

That was fine with me.

day 29

My FIRST NIGHT IN SEG. Officially.

My OIC flipped me the bird with both hands as soon as I walked in. Supposedly, that meant he liked me. He was a skinny guy with close-cropped gray hair, glasses, and a pacemaker. He was a tough old son of a bitch, as they say. Tough like hundred-year-old jerky. He may have looked skinny and bent, but he'd fuck some shit up. Some of the crew called him The Old Man.

I flipped him back with the pocket creeper. Made like I was looking in my pocket for something, but instead of pulling out anything, I flew my middle finger high with a grin on my face.

As soon as I accepted my equipment for the shift—keys, radio, body alarm, and handcuffs—The Old Man shot me in the ass with a rubber band. *Cute. Real fucking cute.* I rolled my eyes. Then one of the other guys aimed for my breast. I'm not a small woman, and neither is my rack.

"Listen, that shit fucking hurts. Not the rack, okay?" I'd put up with all the hijinks, the bitch work, most anything but abuse of the boobs.

Yeah, he didn't listen. With the biggest grin on his face, he shot me in the tit. Then laughed like a maniac. So I took after him. We got into a scuffle right there in the office, me punching him and slamming him into the wall and him laughing and letting me—the rest of the crew watching. Until I broke a coat hook off the wall with his back. That thing clattered to the floor as loud as a gunshot and we froze in place. I was half terrified that when he turned around, part of it would still be hanging out of his back and he'd have a punctured lung. He was fine, but we were both a little in awe.

We'd become friends after I first started on shift, but me kicking his ass seemed to make us family.

After that, he made me my own little rubber band weapon so I could fight with the rest of them. I have to say, I liked the rubber band game better than the fart game. That one was terrible. Especially when I'd have my mouth open to say something, and King Fart would walk behind me and bake one off at just the most opportune moment. Well, I hated it until I figured out I could use the fart game like a gun on the inmates who pissed me off. I could just call one of the guys up the tier, and if I made them stand there with me long enough, they'd gas the whole tier, a practice known as "crop dusting."

My first day, they worked me like a five-dollar whore on a no-limit credit card. An incident had popped off in the chow hall and they'd had to kick people out to make room for the participants. That made us ears deep in property that should have been handled by the shift before. We had six going out and six coming in and all their property had to be searched, documented, and packed up.

When I say searched, I mean we had to look in the spines of books, take apart any electronics, check clothes, make sure items in containers matched the label, physically handle and inspect every item belonging to the inmate. Now, officers are supposed to do this before the property comes to Seg, but while searching incoming property on various occasions, I found hooch (home-made alcohol) made from oranges and Kool-Aid in a shampoo bottle, tobacco, tattoo needles in lamps, and shanks hidden in legal material.

Then before new inmates could be admitted, we have to search the cells, under the door, on top of lights, vents, drawers, every surface or space that could possibly hold contraband. While doing all of that, we still had to keep the cell house running efficiently by taking guys three at a time to the shower—one officer per inmate—and handing out and picking up trays for chow, then monitoring the porters while they cleaned the cell house.

And of course, since I was new meat, the inmates all tucked their heads straight up their asses. They knew I couldn't tell exactly whose voice was whose, so I was serenaded with every filthy thing anyone could think of to say to me, from talking about how when they caught me alone they'd fuck me bloody, cut new holes in me to fuck, or alternately how I was too disgusting to fuck even for a guy who'd been in prison, etc., and so forth. One said something about what a good lay my mother was and asked me how much dick I could take.

They told us in training not to engage them with this sort of behavior and eventually they'd stop. Eventually? Fuck that. I lobbed that last one back. "Probably not as much dick as you."

The whole cell house erupted in laughter and catcalls.

So of course the insults went back to my weight. One asked how much lunch I'd brought and if I had time to be out there on the tier when I had my food waiting for me in the office.

I told them no, I didn't bring a good lunch, and one said, "Girl, don't tell me you don't eat. Not with an ass like that."

"Oh no, punkin. I eat. *I eat good.* In fact, when I get off work tonight, I'm going to the buffet, and I'm going to eat crab legs."

"Ha, I knew it."

I don't even like crab legs. You couldn't pay me enough to put sea spider in my mouth. Or lobster. They look like big water roaches. But when was the last time any of these turds had any crab legs?

"Then I'm going to have some shrimp and steak. Maybe some lobster. A couple glasses of wine. And hell, just because I'm so fucking fat, I'm going to have some pizza too. All cheesy and juicy and…"

By this point the whole cell house had gone quiet. They were listening to me describe food they hadn't had in years, some that a few of them would never have again.

"Fine, we get it. We get it," an inmate whimpered from his cell.

"Oh, do you? I mean, you wanted to talk about what I eat so I thought I'd share. I think I'll be bringing leftovers in my lunch tomorrow. I'll be sure to set the fan at the office door so you can all smell my rib eye, loaded baked potato, and honey-glazed carrots."

They quieted down somewhat, but there were still a few jeers as I walked past. I didn't let it get to me though. I listened. I listened so I could learn the inmates' voices and identify which cells they were coming from, a skill that would serve me well later.

Especially when inmates would scream obscenities at me and then later ask me to fix their cable. "Hmm, I don't see either 'Cunt' or 'Time Warner Cable' on my shirt, so I guess you're shit out of luck."

day 30

"OH NO, THIS CAN'T BE RIGHT, LUNSFORD." THE CAPTAIN'S mustache twitched as he looked through his roster, flipped the pages several times to make sure what he was seeing on the paper wasn't a lie, or to make sure it wasn't going to change the longer he looked at it. "There can't be three women down in Seg. Women don't belong in Seg anyway."

What? Are you kidding me?

The other two women who would be down there with me looked at him as if he'd grown another head.

One day a week, there were three women on shift in Segregation. This was not a new thing. All three of us were hard-asses. We'd all been baptized by fire and come through the other side whole and hearty. None of us took any shit, or were mealy-mouthed about our expectations or treated any one inmate different than another. We were good officers.

But there was our Captain, crying about how unfair it was to the one guy who'd be down there, who would have to stand showers and do any stripouts that came in. Five minutes of nuts and butts while we had to do all of the cell searches and everything else? Cry me a river. Somebody's vag was sandy, but it didn't belong to any one of the three of us.

Everyone backed away from us as we looked at each other, processing. Almost like the way you'd back up from a hungry lion—careful, hoping the predator doesn't notice your movement and pounce.

The relief OIC, a woman in her early fifties, who was like an angry bull when crossed, hopped on it immediately. "Well, since we're just women, why don't you come down to Seg and show us what we're supposed to do? I don't think we can figure it out all by ourselves. Do you?" She turned to look us.

"No, I don't think we can manage," I said. "I have a vagina; therefore, I am incapable of doing my job."

He narrowed his eyes at us, as if there were some doubt as to whether we were serious.

"Lunsford," the male who would be assigned with us said under his breath. "I know you really have a dick. Even if he doesn't."

It made me laugh, but I was still pissed off at what the Captain had said. Not just because it was a slur against women. I can even understand why men didn't trust women as easily as other men in that environment. I'd seen firsthand too many women throw away their careers because some shit bag told them they were pretty.

I didn't like it, but I understood it. But this Captain, he'd seen my work. He knew I was a good officer. He knew the other two were good officers, and he knew we had good, solid reputations.

We discussed it the whole way to the cell house. A couple of inmates from other cell houses yelled greetings to us on our way in and asked us about the weather, how we were doing, just looking to be acknowledged. My OIC told them she didn't know and couldn't figure it out because she was a woman. There were echoes of "fuck that" and "we're fucked" the rest of the walk in. The inmates wanted nothing to do with us when we acted faux helpless. That was the calm before the storm. They knew we were pissed and wanted no part of it.

We hadn't been on duty for fifteen minutes when the first call came asking us what cells we had open for someone who'd popped off at the mouth before shift change. We informed the Captain that we didn't know because we were girls and didn't belong in Segregation. We asked him, in unison, to please send us a big, strong man to help us. When he could locate one.

For women who couldn't do the job, we pulled our own weight in contraband out of the cell house that day. The biggest find was the serrated blade we found in the cell of an inmate known to be HIV positive and who hated officers. It wasn't unheard of for inmates to stick themselves and then use their blood as a weapon.

What scared us wasn't that he'd had it. There was all manner of shit hidden all around the prison at any given time. It was where we were and how he'd gotten it.

Segregation was supposed to be the jail within the jail. It was supposed to be more secure than the rest of the prison. Inmates and their belongings were searched constantly. When inmates were brought into Seg, they were stripped naked and had a flashlight shined up their noses, in their ears, down their throats and up their asses. That blade was too big to be smuggled in the prison wallet (anus).

So either someone hadn't searched his property, or some dirty motherfucker brought it in for him.

day 31

MY MOTHER FINALLY HEARD BACK FROM HER DOCTOR. He suspected cervical cancer. She had to make an appointment to go back in for more tests, but she didn't know how she'd get there because she was in so much pain all of the time that it was hard for her to even get out of bed.

I went in to work and nothing was any better there. For that week I was two days Seg, two days tower, and one day open. This was an open day, and the cell house they put me in had just had an outbreak of scabies.

Fucking scabies.

Scabies are basically skin lice. They're little bugs that burrow and squirm beneath your skin and make you want to rip your own flesh off to stop the itch. They're also highly contagious. You can pick them up by a simple touch or contact.

The whole cell house had to be quarantined and all of the bedding washed, every surface treated. I spent the whole shift drenching myself in hand sanitizer. I felt itchy just being there, but I knew better than to scratch. If I'd accidentally come into contact with any, they could be under my fingernails, or on my fingers or on my skin where I wanted to scratch.

Itching is my Achilles' heel. I'd rather hurt than itch any day.

It wasn't my Friday, but damn. After spending a shift walking around on my tiptoes, a beer couldn't hurt. We went to a bar in the city with a mechanical bull. I remember saying I wasn't going to ride it and I also remember a Hurricane in an orange juice carafe.

Then I remember lying on the floor. No one would ever tell me if I actually rode the bull or not. I don't think I did, but what other reason would I have to be lying on the filthy floor of a bar? Aside from the fact I'd drank three of those Jolly Green Giant-sized Hurricanes?

There were too many people around me, and one guy in particular kept trying to touch me. Before I could knock his teeth out, one of the guys who was with our group, nicknamed Shrek, played knight in shining armor. With one shove, he knocked the guy back several feet and told him to keep his hands off me. He took care of me that night and a couple of others. It was nice to feel like someone really gave a shit about me just because I was me. Not because they felt I owed them something under the hat of wife, mother, daughter, or officer. Not because he was trying to get his dick wet. Because he was my friend. I really needed that. Probably more than I wanted to admit.

day 32

I STARTED MY PERIOD.

While that was not especially spectacular, the part where I sneezed and parted the Red Sea down my pants like Moses kind of was.

I had menorrhagia, which means I bled a lot (no more, thanks to medical procedures); I almost died from it once. Sometimes being a pork chop comes in handy. At the time, the emergency room nurse said if I'd been a smaller woman, I would have bled to death.

I usually kept a clean uniform in the trunk of my car, but today was not a particularly lucky day, and when the Red Storm began, it was ten minutes until I had to be at my post.

I approached the Captain. A different one today than the one who said women didn't belong in Seg. But surprisingly, he would have been the easier sell. He had a wife.

"Captain?"

"Yeah?"

"I need to run home."

"For what?"

"A feminine issue." That should be good enough, right? Everyone knows what that is.

Wrong. "Being?"

"It's that time of the month."

"What time of the month?" Really? I think my mouth fell open.

"Aunt Flo is in town." I tried to be discreet; there were other officers still in the hallway.

"Why the fuck do I care about your Aunt Flo?" He looked at me, a curious look on his face.

Oh. My. God. Are you serious? Really? And I say again, really? At first I thought he was just fucking with me, trying to embarrass me. Until that questioning look on his face didn't merge into a smirk or a laugh. He was serious.

Well, fuck Aunt Flo and fuck him. "I'm on the rag, asshole. *Riding the cotton pony. Plugging it up. Menstruating. Any of this ringing a bell?*"

His whole face turned a rather interesting shade of red, but I refused to be embarrassed. Better him, now, than having that happen on the tier in front of the inmates. That was my biggest fear while I worked there. Not getting shanked, or catching any fucked-up diseases, but bleeding all over myself like a stuck pig in a slaughterhouse.

"You live across town, right? We're short on shift. Just go to the warehouse and get a new uniform."

While that was all fine and dandy, I needed new underwear too. And socks. It had burst down my leg and soaked into my socks.

"Uh, I need things that are not part of my uniform that I have to go home to get."

This time, he caught on and slipped me a twenty to go up the street to K-Mart and buy some underwear and socks.

I made it through K-Mart with my jacket tied around my waist, but I know someone must have seen the big flowering stain of red creeping forward on my thighs. Then I went to the warehouse to get new uniform pants. The warehouse was staffed by inmates, so I wasn't looking forward to this either.

"New pants. Captain should have called."

"I need the old pair," the inmate said.

Oh no, you don't, a little voice in my head whined. *You really don't.* I could feel myself starting to blush, but I shoved that down. I refused to be embarrassed. "I'm wearing them. I'll bring them back after I wash them."

He eyed me for a moment before saying, "No problem, just sign for the new ones." He pushed the paper toward me with a clean, shiny, and kind of starchy brand-new pair of pants.

"Thank you."

"And you don't have to bring them back. We'll just throw them away anyway. No worries."

"Really, thank you."

I shrugged into my new pants and it was quite the feat trying to clean up in the dressing room with nothing but a box of Handi Wipes, but I made it to my post only five minutes late.

Shift was short-staffed, so I got to go down to Seg and be acting Sergeant because I was the only officer in Seg who was regularly assigned to the post. What was especially cool for me was that I knew what I was doing. I was confident in all of my decisions and it was mostly a smooth night.

Except we had an officer down there who didn't think he should have to do what I said because he'd been doing The Job longer and I didn't have a dick. I finally told him in no uncertain terms if he didn't want to do what I asked in my cell house, he was cordially invited to get the fuck out of it. The First Sergeant backed my offer too.

He asked if I was normally such a cunt or if it was because I was on the rag.

I know he meant it to be rhetorical, but I'd already had a fun afternoon of confession, so I figured why the hell not? He asked. He had it coming.

"As a matter of fact, I am." Everyone laughed.

He grabbed the microphone for the PA system. "Attention in the cell house, Lunsford is on the rag. I repeat, *Lunsford is on the rag.*"

You motherfucker. I nodded silently for a moment and smiled before I took the microphone. "And this asshole took my last tampon for his mangina. Apparently, it's sandy. So watch yourselves tonight, gentlemen."

The entire house roared with laughter, but later when I was out on the tier, no one gave me any shit whatsoever.

It turned into a good night.

day 33

I'D BEEN COUNTING DOWN TO MY FRIDAY ALL WEEK. IT HADN'T been a bad week, but I'd worked hard. It was time to unwind.

At this point, I should have seen the pattern in my behavior, and maybe I did. But all I wanted was to be numb. Numb to the job I had, numb to the marriage I didn't, numb to the distance growing between me and my children, numb to the fact my dreams were dying and it looked like this was going to be my life. I had thirty years of this to look forward to.

I'd stopped writing, but I didn't think there was a chance in hell I'd ever make it as a writer anyway. I'd sold several short stories to horror mags, anthologies, and other small venues. Nothing I could make a living from. I'd even finished a romance novel, but it had taken me ten years to do it and I had a bunch of really nice rejection letters. I'd almost wished someone would just tell me I sucked and that it was offensive I ever put fingers to keyboard because then I'd stop trying, stop wishing, stop that awful hope that sometimes felt more like a devouring black hole than encouragement.

But The Job did that for me.

I didn't want to write about knights on white horses, maidens fair, or happily-ever-afters anymore. I didn't want to write about any human relationships because I thought it was all bullshit. There were predators and there were prey. Someone does the fucking, someone gets fucked. Literally and figuratively. End of story.

No, the only thing left to me was the escape I felt when I had a bottle in my hand.

There had come a point in my marriage when I realized I was just hashing off days, waiting to die. I wanted it to be over. And I realized here, in this future I'd made with my newfound freedom, it wasn't any better. I was still miserable and still doing the same thing. Every day was one more that I never had to live again.

That night, I didn't go out with my usual group from work; I went out with a friend of a friend and her crew. She worked law enforcement too and was also going through a divorce. Our situations were very similar.

We went to a cop bar where we talked shop for a good portion of the evening. Everyone laughed while we related stories of some of the dumbest things we'd seen or done. I felt at home with these people, comfortable. I laughed too.

Until someone's ex-wife showed up.

I happened to be sitting by her ex-husband. He and I had gone in together on a "bottomless" pitcher of beer, nothing more nefarious than that, but she lost her goddamn mind.

That's not to say I wasn't considering fucking him. I was. I'd heard my husband was fucking other people. If I was honest with myself, it tore me up like razor wire, just like I knew all the rumors about me hurt him. But for as numb as I wanted to be, there were times I wanted to feel something too. And this guy, he was like me. Neither of us wanted anything but a quick fuck. That's what it would be too. No "making love" or any other bullshit. No strings. Just two people in the dark who never had to look at each other again.

This woman came into the bar screaming. She was short, blond, and skinny with a fake-bake tan and acrylic claws. The friend I'd come with tried to drag me out as soon as she saw her. Told me that she was crazy. I refused to leave. Fuck if I was going to let some bitch I didn't know come in and ruin my night.

Or at least, that's what I said. What I meant was I wasn't going to let some crazy cunt run me out of a bar or off a man. Even if he *used* to be hers. I didn't back down at work, and she could bet her dumpy ass I wasn't going to back down here either.

I had to give this woman points for balls. She had them by the dump truck. I've mentioned it before that I'm not a small woman. I'm six feet without my shoes; I have seven tattoos, shoulders like a linebacker, and a right hook that can knock a man bigger than me on his ass.

But crazy is also said to give people unusual strength.

So when she hit me in the face, it smarted like a motherfucker.

The thing about getting cracked in the chops, though, is after that first contact, your face goes numb. Or maybe that was the adrenaline? I didn't know and I didn't care. I grabbed that pitcher of beer and smashed it into the side of her head. The pitcher was plastic, but I hit her hard enough the pitcher cracked.

The blow sent her flying. It was like watching one of those slobber-knocker punches from *Rocky* in slow motion. Her whole face mashed up like a demented bulldog, there was spittle and blood flying out of her mouth as her head spun to the side, and all the while she seemed to be arching through the air in a Crazy Bitch Cirque de Soleil.

I launched myself up and out of my chair, but the guy caught me. Plucked me from the air like a baseball and jerked me back down into my seat.

"I can't let you do that," he said.

I looked at her and realized how pathetic she was, stalking her ex-husband in a bar and losing her shit all over some woman just sitting by him. A couple people from the group were alternately trying to restrain her from trying to attack me again and cleaning up the blood on her face where her lip had split open.

"You better put your bitch on a leash." I got up from the table and walked to the door.

He followed me. "Hey, uh, give me your number and maybe I can make it up to you?"

Really, asshole? *REALLY?* Still trying to get laid even though his ex had attacked me and he'd stopped me from giving her the ass-kicking she so desperately needed? More proof that men were all the same. Maybe he didn't want to see her get hurt, I rationalized. I could understand that. Even though my husband and I were looking at divorce, I'd never want to see anyone hurt him. But she'd hit me. Pretty fucking hard too.

"No, I don't think so."

"Come on, I thought we were having a good time."

"I've got enough complications. I wasn't looking to exchange numbers. Just fluids. Thanks, but no thanks."

"I, uh, could come over later." His hard mouth turned up in a smile.

Suddenly, everything about him disgusted me. I just wanted to leave. I wanted to go somewhere and just...not be this person. Not have this life. I wanted my husband. I wanted him the way he was when we met. When he loved me. When his embrace had been the shield against the world instead of a cage.

I pulled out my phone and thought about calling him, but I didn't really have anything to say. Because I didn't think he loved me anymore. He didn't even like me. And I didn't even like who he was.

So I just left and walked down the street. My friend picked me up.

"Where are you going, *chica*?" she asked when she pulled up next to me.

We were in the city. I had no fucking clue where I was, where I was going, or how I'd get home. I couldn't say at that point that I gave a fuck.

"I don't know; I just had to get the fuck out of there."

She stopped and opened the door to the truck. "I know another place."

"Yeah, with sturdier pitchers I hope." I climbed in.

"You only hit her once, but you fucked her up." She nodded with approval.

"Not as much as I would've liked," I sighed. I found myself disappointed that I hadn't beaten her until her teeth were spread on the floor like so many Chiclets. Not because she'd hit me, it wasn't her in particular. It was because I wanted to make someone hurt like I hurt. I wanted to unleash my rage on someone and send it home with them. I didn't want it anymore.

"I need another beer."

That was the only thing that made me happy. At the bottom of a pitcher, there was a hazy warmth that wasn't a hot rage or a cold chill. It didn't *hurt*. Being drunk was like cuddling up with a plush blanket.

"Don't we all?" she sighed and put the truck in gear.

I knew she was going through a tough time too, but she didn't seem inclined to talk about it and I wasn't inclined to push. I figured if she wanted to talk, she was a big girl wearing her big-girl knickers and could tell me what she wanted me to know, and otherwise, it wasn't my business. And she hadn't really tried to get in mine. I hadn't really spilled all my guts to her. I'd just told her I was separated and she'd understood.

We drove back to town and went to a local dive where the darts and pool were cheap, and where we knew most of the patrons already. She got some guy she ended up going home with to buy us drinks all night.

When she left with him, I walked home.

I hated every second of that walk. I didn't have any music to listen to, nothing pressing to occupy my brain, and my buzz had faded a half an hour before I left. It was just me, alone in my head. It sucked and I wanted to be drunk.

My apartment building loomed before me and it seemed an impossible task to trudge up those stairs alone, go to my empty apartment, and just...sit.

I called my tower rat friend who came over and brought a really big bottle of bourbon, and we did shots until we passed out on my couch.

day 34

MY KIDS DIDN'T WANT TO SEE ME ON THE WEEKEND. They both had other things they wanted to do. The oldest was doing something with my dad and the youngest said she was sick.

I went over and spent an hour or so with my mother. That was as long as she could stand up. We didn't talk about anything. We sat together while she flipped back and forth between football, the home shopping channel, and CNN. I left when she went to bed. I could have waited for my older daughter, but if she didn't think it was worth seeing me, then why should I bother?

I spent the rest of the day alone and I didn't like it. Too much time with my own head again. I chatted with some people on-line. Tried to write, but I didn't have anything to say. The stories that used to live in my head were gone.

In the end, the only thing I wanted to do was drink some more. I went over to a friend's house, the same one who'd come over the night previous. We got shit-faced and played video games for hours. At three in the morning, he called his girl-friend, who was also an officer, to go get us Burger King.

If I'd been her, I would have told him to go fuck himself and have the bitch he was with go get him his damn Burger King. But this poor girl had no self-respect. None at all. She'd been asleep when he called and she got up out of bed to drive twenty minutes to Burger King, which was actually within walking distance of my friend's house.

She even paid for our food.

And when she dropped it off, that's all it was. He answered the door, took the bag from her, and said, "Thanks, babe." *Then he closed the door.*

He didn't even invite her inside.

I could see her through the window, still standing on the porch, confused. As if she almost wasn't sure where she was or what was going on. She started crying, but she let him get away with it.

That disgusted me thoroughly. It almost put me off my food. Almost.

"That's fucked up, man," I said.

"I know, right?" he said, laughing.

"You're an asshole."

"And this is news how?"

I laughed. I couldn't help it. "You treat her like a doormat."

"She lets me." He shrugged.

"I'm going to take her under my wing. Just you wait." I took another bite of my burger. "But damn it's nice to have Burger King delivery whenever I want it."

"Ain't it?" He smirked and shoved another beer at me.

I drank half in one gulp. "I don't know. It makes me curious what else you could make her do."

"Now you're thinking. Come up with some ideas. I'll try a few."

I shouldn't have laughed. I should have had more empathy for that poor, naïve girl, but I didn't. I still thought it was all predator/prey and if she wanted to be prey, who was I to stop her?

He'd invited me to crash on the couch, but his sister had a

friend crashing too and she'd taken the good couch. The cats had christened the other one, so I crept out at dawn when I was sober enough to drive.

I called her the next day and asked her why she put up with that shit and she said because she knew he really loved her, which only reinforced my predator/prey ideology because right after that, she asked me if I thought he was cheating on her.

Nothing ever happened between me and my friend, but you can bet your ass I wouldn't put up with some female friend spending the night with my man. And I wouldn't fetch and carry them anything but a Molotov cocktail.

day 35

THE DOCTOR'S OFFICE HAD CALLED AND CONFIRMED THAT my mom had cancer, but she could have a hysterectomy and there was a high survival rate, so we had every reason in the world to be hopeful. She was supposed to go in for tests for her surgery, but she didn't feel well enough to go and rescheduled.

I can't count how many times she canceled those pre-hysterectomy tests because she'd get dizzy, or had a panic attack, or she'd just be in too much pain to function. I didn't understand with her level of illness, her disabilities, why they didn't admit her to the hospital to do the tests and keep her sedated until they could operate. She was in so much pain.

Unless all of her screaming was simply histrionics, but I didn't think that was the case.

Looking at her lying in bed, a small, shriveled lump, crying and afraid, I realized my mom had gotten old. Not just in years, because mid-sixties wasn't really old, but in her soul.

Speaking of histrionics…I know that's kind of an over-wrought description, but she seemed so weak and frail. So broken. Soul-weary.

There were times as a kid that I thought she really hated me and I thought I really hated her. I said I wasn't going to bad-mouth her and I won't—I will own all of the bad things I did too. I freely admit that I was a horrible teenager and I put my mother through so many things that I didn't need to. I'd decided I was an adult at sixteen and that was that.

But I have to give some examples of her behavior here too, so you understand why our relationship was so strained.

Once, she got angry at me and threw the toothbrush holder I made in ceramics class so it shattered on the floor, then made me clean it up. It was ugly, this sick swirl of green and yellow paint smears, but I'd made it for her. I cried and I don't remember exactly what she said, but I remember thinking that she seemed glad to have hurt me. I decided then that I would never show her how anything she did caused me pain. No matter what she did, I wouldn't care.

For a long time, I didn't. Even when she told me she wanted to kill herself—that she should just go jump off the bridge. I told her I'd drive her so she didn't leave the car and to either do it or shut the fuck up about it.

When I was sixteen, she was trying to teach me how to drive. She told me to parallel park in a space I wasn't comfortable with, I told her I didn't want to try it and she started screaming at me. So I screamed back. She slapped me across the face so hard my head hit the glass while the car was moving. I hauled off and slapped her right back. She threatened to call the police, and I didn't give a shit one way or another. I told her that was fine, but if she laid hands on me again she'd get more of the same.

There were a few times when that got me kicked out of the house. Some were deserved, others weren't. I'd decided I was going to do what I wanted to do when I wanted to do it, and there was nothing anyone could say or do to stop me. I lived on my own for a while when I was sixteen. I actually went to class and did my homework when I was only accountable to myself.

Once, I even told her that I wished she'd never adopted me and she said she did too because I had bad genes and I'd never be anything. We were good at hurting each other.

But this was still the woman who'd waited seven years for a baby. For me. They'd gotten the call for a baby before me and they hadn't taken her. My mother said she didn't feel right for them, but when she met me, she and my dad both knew I was the one. I was theirs.

This was still the woman who taught me my phonics in the bath, kissed my cuts, and always made sure I had every piece of clothing I ever wanted, every toy I coveted, had the best birth-day parties and made my birthday practically a national holiday while she went without. I had two cars before I was eighteen and my mother never had one that she could say was only hers.

When I told her I was pregnant with my oldest daughter, I was nineteen and jobless, living with my parents. She didn't get angry like I thought she would, given that when she found a condom in my purse in high school, she called me all manner of nasty names.

Pregnant was different somehow, maybe because I was sup-posed to be an adult. She was comforting and helpful, even when I told her I might put the baby up for adoption. A mom? Shit. How could I be a mom at nineteen? I couldn't handle my own life, let alone anyone else's. This whole other innocent little person…

My father walked the halls with me for nineteen hours while I was in hard labor. My mother was the one who went to Lamaze class with me and held my hand while I was in labor even though she'd been sick with the flu.

When my husband and I had separated, there was never any question that I would move in with my parents, and my mother had offered to watch the kids for me while I looked for a job. She'd come in and pet my hair and my back while I bawled; sobbed like I was dying when I heard my husband had slept with someone else after we separated. (I know, such a double standard. I hated that it hurt me, I didn't want to feel anything else for him.)

Even as sick as she was now, she was still trying to keep up with my kids and taking care of them because I couldn't.

Or wouldn't.

Maybe I didn't even know how to be a mom then.

All of this matters because it tangled like some rancid ribbon around what I felt for my mother. It was complicated.

Part of me wanted to hurt her back now that she was weak, and part of me wanted to curl up around her and beg her not to leave me alone in the world because I wasn't ready. I was still just a little girl playing dress-up and house.

I lay down with her for a while and read a book. I didn't say any of the things that were on the tip of my tongue. It was swollen from too much salt anyway.

day 36

THE PRISON CALLED ME TO SEE IF I WANTED OVERTIME, SO I went. I had to get ahead on my bills. I was renting furniture and spending way too much at the bar.

I should have stayed home.

I was happy they decided to put me in Seg. If I could have been down there five days a week instead of two, I would have been all over it. But the place was rocking and rolling and had been all day. A bunch of guys had just come in from the Medium for dumping boiling oil on another inmate's face. They stole the oil from the kitchen and set it to boil in someone's hot pot. Then they waited for their target. Someone told me that the inmate's face had melted away with the oil, running down his neck with the hot grease. I didn't quite believe it; I imagined it would have to blister first and I didn't think the hot pot could get it quite that hot.

First thing I did when I got to Seg was walk around and ask who wanted showers. I was told if guys were asleep not to wake them up. They knew what time we took names for showers. It was their responsibility to make sure they washed their own asses. For the most part, I agreed with that. No one got me up to wash my ass, and my shirt said Department of Corrections not Concierge.

But I would always bang on their cell door a couple of times.

It made more work for us, but I didn't want to smell these guys. If they didn't make it to shower call, they usually didn't bother to "birdbath" it either. (Meaning they would run water in their sink and bathe. Like a birdbath.)

One guy didn't wake up. I could see he was breathing, so I went on about my safety check and shower call.

About halfway through the showers, the guy who'd slept through the call woke up pissed off. He asked if he could please get a shower. I said no. We had to treat them all the same. If I made an allowance for him, I'd have to make it for everyone. Part of prison is learning to follow rules and enduring the consequences when you don't. We're correcting (hence corrections) the idea that the rules don't apply to these individuals, and we're forcing them to function in a societal setting and to deal with consequences.

He was running off at the mouth and being a general pain in my ass. I couldn't make it any clearer to him that I wasn't his alarm clock and I wasn't going to be. He said he was going to tie a string to his toe next time so I could pull it and wake him up.

What?

Then he said he wanted us to practice. He hadn't heard all of my 534 versions of no, so I finally said that yes, on my next time around the tier we could practice.

So when I came back around, he'd positioned himself the other way on his bunk, facing the door. He had his blankets pulled up to his chin. (Remember, it was still like ninety to a hundred degrees inside.) A length of some nylon thread, like fishing line, hung out of his cell.

I just knew he'd tied it to his dick. I don't know how I knew, but I did.

"Are you ready to practice?" he asked me with a big grin. "Just tug it a little."

If I could have rolled my eyes any harder, they might have fallen out of my face. I decided to give him a chance not to be a dumbass. "I don't think we need to practice because I'm not going to pull that string to wake you up for a shower. You're a grown man."

"No, we have to practice. You said you would."

I had at that. I'd said we'd practice because I wanted him to shut the fuck up. I always did what I said I'd do. Always.

"It's not too late to change your mind. I'm too busy to worry about gentle tugs."

He laughed. "But, Sarge, you're a woman. How hard could it be?"

"Okay, well, are you sure it's tied to your toe?"

He nodded enthusiastically. So I gathered the length in my fist. "Are you ready?" He nodded some more.

I jerked that thing so hard it snapped. As I suspected, he'd tied the string to his dick.

I've never heard such a sound come out of a man before or since. Or seen someone fly the way he flew through the air. It was like his bunk was a toaster and he was a Pop-Tart for all of one second that seemed to last minutes.

Then he was on the floor naked and writhing.

"Was that good? Would that wake you up?" When he didn't answer, I spoke again. "What's wrong? Do you need to go to the clinic?"

"No, ma'am," he choked out.

Asshole. Maybe he'd think twice about inflicting his dick and dumbassery on the next officer. I went about my business of searching cells.

I'd thought I already had my excitement for the day, but I wasn't so lucky. I was flipping through an inmate's address book when I found an address and a phone number I recognized. It belonged to the clinic secretary.

Now, I knew there were ways for anyone to get this information. The fact that he had it didn't necessarily mean she'd given it to him, but it was something I had to report. If not for her safety, then for the rest of the staff.

I confiscated the address book as evidence.

I didn't want to think she was dirty, but a gnawing hole in my gut said she was.

And I hadn't been wrong yet.

This guy was a real piece of shit too. He had something like fourteen counts of child molestation and kidnapping. He'd been pimping girls under the age of fourteen. I believe he was an enforcer for the Bloods.

He later ended up convincing a female officer to have a relationship with him. She was in my training class and I can't say I was surprised. I didn't like her from day one. There was something false about her, this faux piety. Her kids went to school with mine and I had to tell them they couldn't be friends with her son.

Not only because we'd ejected her from our world, but having a relationship with someone in your care like that is a sex crime. Of course, then there's the part where she had gotten him a lawyer and was trying to get his sentence reduced and wanted him to come live with her and her children. If she'd wantonly and actively seek to bring that into her home, what else had her poor children been exposed to?

There was a little justice in the world though. This inmate had priapism, meaning he'd gotten an erection that didn't go away. He refused to allow them to operate to relieve the condition. Bottom line? He ended up with gangrene and had to catheterize himself several times a day.

day 37

THERE WAS AN "INCIDENT" ON DAY SHIFT. A FIGHT IN ONE of the cell houses had spilled out into the street. A few friends of mine were hurt. Nothing severe; everyone walked away from the encounter, but it drove the point home how fast things could change, and "what if" was on everyone's mind.

Corrections officers have to ask that question a hundred times a day in as many different incarnations.

What if this inmate…

What if this officer…

What if I screw up and another officer doesn't go home?

What if *I* don't go home?

We have to imagine every possible answer to those questions and plan for every contingency.

Then we have to act like the answers to those questions don't matter so we can do our jobs. So when we go home, we can leave the remnants of the prison at the gate behind us, and our loved ones can forget we ask ourselves those questions so they don't have to ask them either.

day 46

I WAS THE SICKEST I'D EVEN BEEN IN MY LIFE.

I'd felt like crap the night before, but I'd still gone out with everyone. I'd read that somebody used Jaeger as cough syrup. So I drank eight Jaeger Bombs, and that sore throat I'd been nursing felt fantastic.

The next day? Not so much.

I was sitting at Exit/Entry, the point in the Maximum unit where staff would come in and out of the prison, and every time I coughed, it felt like someone was scraping out the inside of my chest with a sharp rock. I was burning up, sweating like a whore in church, then I was cold, shivering. But Exit/Entry was by the front door. People kept coming and going out. I had a space heater on my feet. So I didn't think I had a fever until the tiles on the floor started moving on their own.

Once, when I'd been sick like that before, I'd been watching a documentary on the Valentine's Day Massacre. When the reenactment started and the report of the tommy guns echoed through the speakers, I hit the deck because I thought I was actually being shot at. Prison and hallucinations weren't a good mix, so I knew I had to go home.

Just as I was going to call the Captain, I saw another officer leaving. He winked at me and said he was going home sick. Bastard. He wasn't sick.

I coughed again, sounding like a barking dog, and I couldn't stop. One of the special teams guys took one look at me coming through the entry point and said he was going to get the Captain.

The Captain cocked his head to one side to look at me sprawled halfway on the desk and asked if I was going to make it. By that point, I couldn't even answer him. They called my husband to come and get me.

I had to go to the doctor to get cleared to return to work. Which I didn't get for a week. I had strep. I'd thought I was just being a pussy about seasonal allergies.

day 55

I FLEW TO PORTLAND FOR SUNSHINE'S WEDDING AND ENDED
up losing my driver's license on the concourse. That meant I
wasn't able to rent a car, so I had to call my friend to come pick
me up from the airport. I was embarrassed to have to inflict
myself on her when she had so much going on.

But she came to get me with a smile, and even though she
hadn't planned on me staying with her, she and her husband-to-
be happily made a place for me in their home.

I didn't sleep that night; I was worried how I was going to
get home. Back when I worked for an airline, if you lost your
ID, you were fucked. You weren't flying anywhere. I tried not to
focus on it, to remember this weekend wasn't about me, but my
friend, and her wedding and beautiful family.

Yet again, I had to call my husband and ask him to help me.
He was on the phone with people all day trying to figure out
how to get me on that plane or if he was going to have to drive
up to get me.

Sunshine got married outside in this beautiful park and the
reception was a campout. I'd never camped out before, and I still
haven't. I ended up leaving before the campout began because I
had no way to get back to the airport in time for my flight the next
day. The bride's mom let me hitch a ride with her back to her hotel
and I got a room there so I could take the shuttle to the airport.

The bride was beautiful, radiant. I know they always talk about glowing, but she did. She does. I was so happy for her and her husband. They just fit together perfectly like two puzzle pieces.

The beer was provided by the groom, handcrafted. It may have been the best beer I've ever had, but it was lost on me because I kept drinking until my face went numb. I danced for hours, jamming with the DJ. At one point, I realized I was up dancing by myself and I didn't care. It felt so good and I felt free.

I'm surprised I didn't puke my free all over the place and embarrass myself further, but I wasn't the only one who'd indulged in more than they should have.

But for all of that, there was a serenity to that place that spoke to me, and I fell in love with Portland, with the clear water, the majestic trees, and the people. The people there were so open, warm, and kind. All but the security guard who wouldn't go back on the concourse and grab my ID for me when I could see it through the gate. Who also couldn't be bothered to tell me I didn't need my ID to fly. All I had to do was walk through something they called "the sniffer."

The sniffer posed its own set of problems because it analyzed your hair and skin, sniffing out whatever chemicals you'd been exposed to, and then you'd be processed accordingly. I knew I hadn't been in contact with any—oh. Right.

I had gunpowder residue on my hands from the firing range. CS gas. Who knew what else from the contraband I'd handled before I left?

When the screener asked what I'd been exposed to, I gave him a list of known culprits. As he was reading down the piece of paper I'd handed him, I'd watched the expression on his face shifting from bored to holy-shit-it's-a-live-one.

He was crestfallen when I told him it was for my job. They

actually called the human resources department at the prison to verify I was employed with them and had been exposed to these chemicals within the scope of my duties.

My husband took me out to lunch when I came back. We didn't talk about anything but work. It was the only safe topic.

day 58

I DECIDED TO GET A NEW TATTOO.

A large raven on my bicep with its head turned to watch my back.

The raven had come to be representative of so many things to me that it just felt right. The raven has many meanings throughout world religions, from Odinism and Asatru to Native American beliefs, Celtic mythologies, Islam, and even Christianity.

For me, I felt a special kinship with the Celtic representation and the Morrigan—the goddess of battle, strife, and fertility. Essentially, hearth and war. The duality of her dominion I felt was very representative of me. The two people I had to be—one behind the walls and the one outside.

Some stories portray her as a triplicate goddess, like the fates, and the maiden, the mother, and the crone. I like that too. The third option, the person who I could grow into who didn't have to be hearth or war, but could be both. The other two will always be part of me, but I don't have to be one or the other.

One of the aspects of the Morrigan's realm is rebirth. That was my goal. To be me again. To find myself and not to ever lose me again. To be reborn strong and whole.

The Morrigan is one hell of a wingman to be watching your back.

I spent three hours in the chair and every time the needle

pierced my skin, I reminded myself why I wanted this tattoo. What it meant to me and the person I wanted to be—and I guess it was only fitting that after marking myself as a warrior woman that I was put to the test.

I had to earn my mark.

day 70

A QUIET DAY IN SEG—THE SHOWERS HAD JUST BEEN painted, so no one would be coming out of their cells.

And obviously, we then had too much time on our hands.

The officers in Seg had always been big with the pranking or outright fuckery. It was our coping mechanism. I had one uniform shirt I never wore anywhere but Seg because I'd been sprayed with bleach so many times. There were a few of us who had those same streaked shirts. We'd have bleach wars, sneaking up on one another with the spray bottles of bleach. It was like prison paintball.

One of the guys almost got divorced because I wrote my name on the back of his neck with a red Sharpie and squirted him with my flowery scented hand sanitizer. I really thought he'd notice me writing on him while he was on the phone, but he was oblivious. That's what he got for hiding my lunch box.

Once, I made the mistake of leaving my radio on the desk when I went to the bathroom. I was wrong to leave it on the desk, and my coworkers showed me just how wrong by taking it apart and hiding the pieces all over the office.

But none of these compared to the day we took an industrial roll of plastic wrap and bound one of the corporals to a pillar just inside the entrance. Of course, we had contingency plans. If something had popped off, we had a multitool we could have used to slice him free in about a minute. And where we'd bound him, no inmates could see him.

The officer was a willing participant.

Just like the one we'd tied into The Chair the week before. The Chair was a restraint tool used to calm inmates when they won't settle down. Since we can't shoot them up with Thorazine like they did in the old days, we strap them in a special chair where their hands and feet are bound and they can't move, and that's where they stay until they stop fighting, spitting, throwing shit (literally), or being a general danger to themselves or the facility. Some dipshit in Illinois didn't follow proper procedure and killed an inmate with The Chair, though, so the administration didn't let us use it often. Which pissed me off. Watching shows like *Lock Up* and *Jail*, you see a guy start popping off—acting like he doesn't want to comply, mouthing off, spitting, or other combative behavior—and they slap his ass in The Chair. They'd gain compliance in a couple hours. I think it's good risk reduction when done properly and humanely.

Anyway, our First Sergeant sat down in it to teach us how to do the restraints in accordance with policy. He actually had us tie him up. He should have known better. When we had the last restraint in place, the three of us looked at each other and grinned. Suddenly, the First Sergeant knew where he'd fucked up. But this guy was the king of the prank. He was the one who would throw rocks at the sensors on the fence so it would set off an alarm and patrol would have to come investigate it. His employee file was probably six inches thick with only the things he'd been caught doing. His exploits were legendary. We knew he'd appreciate it on a certain level if we left him there…

So we did.

We left him secured in The Chair in the storage room/bathroom, laughing like hyenas the whole time. Only for about a half an hour, though. The inmates would know otherwise.

I was elected to let him out because the rest of the crew knew he wouldn't lay into me like he would them because we were good friends outside of work. But he was laughing when I released the restraints.

The officer we'd bound to the pillar, now, we left him there longer than a half an hour. It had taken at least that long to bind him properly, so we had to get our investment back and make a profit, right? We only ended up leaving him there for an hour, though, because we had other things to do. We decided since no one was coming out for a shower, we'd go ahead and pull a few guys out and toss their houses looking for contraband. Nothing interesting was found, but not for lack of trying.

I actually liked searching cells. I thought it was like a game of hide-and-seek. They tried to hide things from me and I had to seek it. If I didn't find it, they won, but if I did, I won.

By the end of the day, even with that, I was actually bored. So I started cleaning out the drawers in the desk and organizing the office. I found the night shift's pack of playing cards so I cut out the part in the employee handbook about playing cards, reading magazines, etc., and I taped it on the front of the pack and put it back where I found it.

day 71

THE NEXT DAY THERE WAS A NOTE ON THE PACK OF CARDS that said, "Fuck You." So I cut them all up in little pieces and then put them back in the box. And my whole crew and I laughed hysterically while I did it.

It was amazing I found the time to sit down to cut up those cards because apparently we had to pay for all the fun we'd had the day before. The place was like a madhouse.

To begin, I had a newbie to train. He meant well, but he was slower than a box of hair. He was also afraid of the inmates. Not a good combination. Especially when one of the cells we had to search for the day belonged to a serial killer who was special management inside of special management. He was in Segregation not for something he'd done but because he was so charismatic, he couldn't be permitted out in general population. When officers spoke to him, we had to do it in pairs, and the brass preferred they be Sergeant and above.

The inmate obviously had severe OCD. Everything in his cell was just so. He even had three salt packets and three pepper packets arranged exactly two millimeters apart. I know because I was curious enough to measure it. When he put his playing cards away, they were in order by suit. The other officer was afraid to touch anything.

"What if he knows I was going through his things?" he asked me.

I rolled my eyes and asked for deliverance from dumb-shittery. "Of course he knows you went through his things. This is prison." I found myself using that phrase to explain things more and more.

"But what if he's mad?" His eyes were wide and he reminded me of a rabbit.

"So the fuck what? He's an inmate. It's his job to hide shit and it's yours to find it. Do your job. I can guarantee you that he did his."

I really thought he was going to cry. I think if I'd held a gun to his head, he might have still had to think about whether he was going to touch this inmate's property. Now, usually, I treat an inmate's cell with respect. Still, I'm not going to let that interfere with my job. I usually tried to put things back where the inmate had left them, but if it wasn't perfect, I wasn't going to cry about it. I had to finish searching the cell myself and I found nothing but nuisance contraband, so I confiscated that. I did put his playing cards back in the pack out of order and I thought this officer was going to cry again, but I did it for training purposes. The inmate never said shit to me about it. He accepted it was just part of prison. And the officer, well, he didn't last very long.

The guy in the next cell had more than two hundred pictures. I told him after he got back from his shower he needed to mail some home. Now, I didn't have to do that. I could have chosen which fifty he got to keep and sent the rest to Property, where they would have been mailed home at his expense. Some officers would do that, picking the crappiest, least meaningful pictures that they could to let the guy keep.

He tried to argue with me, like I knew he would. They all do. I discussed it with him for a half an hour, again, something else I didn't have to do. Policy said fifty pictures. Period. Finally, I'd had enough and told him to send them out or I would.

The trays for chow arrived and after we'd passed about half of them, the house started rocking again, bunks banging, screaming. I asked one of the guys what the problem was—turned out they'd been shorted their cookie.

Food isn't just food in prison. It's the stuff of riots and shit bombs. I wasn't about to take all that nonsense because some dumbshit in the kitchen forgot to put cookies on the trays. I finished passing the rest of my trays, then made an announcement on the mic that I would be on the phone with the kitchen to get their cookies directly.

The Lieutenant had just come in for the post check as I made the announcement and he was talking to the First Sergeant when I made the call.

"This is Lunsford in Seg. The trays were missing the cookies," I told the food service supervisor.

"No, they weren't."

I sighed. "Yes, they were. I passed the trays myself. Saw there were no cookies on the trays."

"I put them on there myself."

Highly fucking unlikely since I'd passed the trays myself and checked each one. "Well, then the inmates you sent with the trays ate them on the way over. *Send the cookies.*"

"I can't do that."

"Listen to me very fucking closely. If you think I'm going to get hit with a piss bomb because you don't want to give us the cookies, you are sadly fucking mistaken. My guys will get their cookies. They have them coming. If you don't have those over here in ten goddamn minutes, I'm going to come to the kitchen and get them myself. I can promise you, if I have to leave my post to come over there, you will not fucking like it. *Bring me the goddamn cookies.*" I slammed the phone down.

Through the whole exchange, the Lieutenant had been motioning for me to give him the phone. After I hung up, he laughed. "Why didn't you give me the phone? That's what I'm for."

"I don't need you to handle my business."

"Obviously." He looked at me and we both laughed, realizing that I'd just said the same thing to him I said to inmates when they offered me "protection."

The food service supervisor's supervisor called. He said he didn't appreciate how I'd talked to his employee, his employee was very upset, and he threatened to talk to the Lieutenant. I told him the Lieutenant had been standing right next to me the whole time.

We got our cookies.

That wasn't the end of the bullshit though. The new guy had been threatened. An inmate he'd made angry had threatened to shank him, and that meant an immediate transfer to a slam cell—a regular cell that had an extra door that further segregated inmates from staff and other inmates. The inmate promptly refused and we had to do a Force Cell Move. Since the inmate refused to come out to be moved, our special team had to suit up in riot gear and go in and get him, which was always a pain in the ass, but we were lucky he wasn't one who liked to play in his own waste. Some guys, out of sheer perversity, would slather themselves in their own shit to make it harder for the officers to get a good grip on them.

Then we had to make two more moves because two guys

got rolled from the Medium and we had to deal with their property. I found hooch—homemade alcohol—in a VO5 shampoo bottle in one of the boxes of property. At first sniff, it even smelled good, almost like some fruity shampoo. But the label on the bottle didn't match the scent and there was a bit of a tang to the scent. So I called for a testing kit to verify the alcohol content.

We had to make more moves in the cell house because the inmate in possession of the hooch had to be moved to a slam cell too. All he would get was a paper dress for the first twenty-four hours and he'd be behind a slam door—what Segregation should actually be like.

It's called Segregation for a reason—the inmates are segregated from the rest of the population and from each other. Seg is supposed to be solitary and isolated, but our Segregation unit was more like a regular cell house, with the restriction that the inmates never got to come out of their cells unless it was for their hour of rec time or their shower. They weren't really solitary and isolated unless they'd earned time in one of the slam door cells, but we only had a few of those.

It wasn't until much later in the evening that I finally was able to sit down and write the disciplinary report. I came out of the office to get another officer to sign as witness and it looked like a tornado of picture bits had exploded outside a cell, the one with the inmate whom I'd told to mail out his pictures. And they smelled like piss. So rather than mail out his pictures and keep fifty, he'd torn them *all* up and pissed all over them. *His* pictures. That another inmate would have to clean up.

How did this punish me exactly? I'd already had a hard day, and if he wanted his cell to smell like piss, it was no skin off my ass. In fact, if he stunk up the whole cell house, it was possible the next time he was in general population, he'd get his ass kicked. So again, what did that have to do with me?

day 73

SOMETIMES I WAS SCHEDULED TO LISTEN TO INMATE PHONE calls. Every single call inmates made were recorded and had to be reviewed. It didn't always suck, but most days an anal yeast infection was more fun. Although, sometimes, it was better than *General Hospital*.

First on the docket was the same serial killer whose cell I'd searched the day before. I didn't want to know that his wife could fit the cordless phone all the way into her vagina. Or the sound it made into the phone as she did so, like stirring macaroni. I didn't want to know that it hurt her, but she did it because he got off on the control he had over her. She obviously didn't understand he was getting off on her pain too. He wanted to be told everything she was wearing, but he wanted to hear about the brands. Ralph Lauren sheets. DKNY nightshirt. Some Italian underwear. Her voice was so high-pitched and vacuous. It gave me a headache just to hear her speak. She so obviously had no clue if this guy ever got out he'd kill her. Probably with phones in her vagina.

It was also interesting to note that she'd married him and not told her parents. She was going to a friend's house later because they'd be home, so he should call her there. Nothing really interesting to write down and report.

The first half of the next phone call was in Spanish, so I made a note to get a translator to listen to the call. Sometimes, they'd speak in another language if they were talking about things they didn't want us to understand. About halfway through this call, though, they switched back to English and it was more sex. That was all these fuckers talked about. Sex. Drugs. How the man is keeping them down.

I almost felt bad for this guy. He was talking to his girlfriend about what their first time was going to be like when he got out, and he was telling her how much he missed her, how much he wanted her. She got down and dirty and asked him for details. She wanted him to measure his dick. So he did, and when he told her it was six inches hard, there was dead silence on the line. He asked her if it made her hot, if it's a good length. More silence and then she scrambled to reassure him it was a good length, but he wouldn't be soothed.

The next call was an inmate who I know had at least three women putting money on his account so he could buy things through the prison store. The woman he was calling didn't answer right away, so the first thing he wanted to know was what she was doing that she was too busy to accept his call. They fought, on her dime, for an hour. He accused her of fucking everyone from the bum on the corner to his brother. The kicker came when she admitted that she had, in fact, been banging his brother blue and she was sucking him off when this guy called.

I spit out my coffee and half snorted it out my nose. The inmate lost his shit like some rabid baboon. He said he'd kill her when he got out, that he was going to find a way to get out before his release date and she wouldn't know when or where it'd happen, only that he would. He talked about lighting her on fire and doing obscene things to her dead body.

I had to give this woman credit. Rather than be afraid, she

told him if he lit her on fire, he wouldn't have a dead body left to do obscene things to and he should really rethink his strategy. And that if he'd been a man and had a real job to begin with, he'd be taking care of her instead of sitting in prison, letting other women take care of him. While he was still trying to understand what was happening, she drove it home and called him a pussy and said that's why she was with a real man, and then hung up the phone.

So I guess she'd found out about the other women. He'd be a real peach the next few days.

He was also an escape risk. He'd made criminal threats against this woman. I had to document it and turn it in, which meant he'd probably be coming to Seg. It was going to be hard not to point and laugh at him because he got told, as they say.

day 89

MY MOM FINALLY WENT IN FOR HER TESTS AND THEY
scheduled her surgery. We discovered later that Dilly,
my parents' dog, had developed ovarian cancer around the same
time. We lost Dilly.

It's kind of crazy and makes no sense, but sometimes I wondered if Dilly did that for my mother, if she went through it so
my mother could survive it. It's stupid, but I wanted to believe
it then and I still want to now, I guess to give shape and form to
the chaos. To have proof of some higher power even if it's just
the love of an animal for her human.

The treatment plan for my mother was a full hysterectomy
and then more tests to see if they needed to do chemotherapy.
My mother had been expecting worse. Her mother had fought
breast cancer for a long time, beginning with lump removal all
the way to a double mastectomy.

My mom was still afraid, we all were, but there was strength
in knowing a fix for her pain loomed on the horizon.

And I felt like an asshole all over again for leaving her alone.
I wanted to apologize, but I still didn't know how. I mean, I
could open my mouth, I could say the words, but would they
mean anything to her?

I'd stopped arguing with her about every little thing, even
when I knew I was right. She didn't have to agree with me for

me to be right. I didn't have to shove my thoughts down her throat and I didn't have to let her shove hers down mine. It wasn't worth the shouting matches and the upset it caused both of us.

If she said something I didn't like, I'd ask her to let it go, and if she wouldn't, I just got up and left. Disengaged.

I knew she'd never change her mind on anything, and neither would I. So what was the point in arguing? I didn't have enough energy to keep banging my head against a brick wall.

day 91

THERE WAS ANOTHER INCIDENT AT WORK, BUT STILL NO big blowup like we'd been expecting. It goes like that sometimes, always in a state of flux. It waxes and wanes like the moon, but unlike the moon, it can't be marked on any regular schedule.

This time it was inmate on officer.

It happened in the chow hall, with all the makings of a riot. Some of the officers on scene didn't respond as they should have. You would have thought they'd be spoiling for a fight. But one of the fucking yard officers just stood there, frozen. Worthless. While an inmate assaulted one of the guys in black. A blacksuit. The blacksuits were supposed to be our elite crew, almost like a SWAT team.

And he knocked him smooth the fuck out.

The prison went on lockdown.

Which is what one would expect, right? But it wasn't a true lockdown. No, it was only lockdown for guys who didn't have jobs. The inmates who worked private industry jobs, the jobs in which the prison could make money on their labor and the jobs for which certain parties got paid bonuses, they got to still go to work. Which was about half of the Max. So it wasn't really lockdown. And they wondered why morale was low, why there was such a high turnover of staff. Why officers gave up and got lazy, not bothering to do more than maintain the status quo. Yeah, there's a clue. It was obvious what's important to them.

At the fed, if staff is assaulted, they go on lockdown for a minimum of two weeks. No visitors for any inmates, no religious callouts, no activities, nothing. They mean what they say. Is it any wonder they look at the state officers and snicker behind their hands or just outright pity them?

Not only was it an insult to staff, it sent the message to the inmates that they could do whatever the fuck they wanted and they'd get away with it. Great way to stand behind your team, to build a strong herd where no one feels like maybe the inmates really do care more about you than your fellow staff.

day 92

SHITASS REPERCUSSIONS ASIDE, I'D DECIDED THIS WAS GOING to be my career. So I bitched about it along with everyone else, but I kept going to work. That's what you do in corrections, you go to work. We'd talked about protesting and staging a walkout, but we all knew no one would do that.

You're sick. Go to work.

You're dying. Go to work.

You're dead. Get your bitch ass up and go to fucking work.

All of the pressure we're under, the body adjusts. It's when the body realizes it doesn't have to function under that kind of stress that it says "fuck you" and promptly starts shutting down.

My father had two years of sick leave and vacation built up when he retired from the fed. He woke up one day and just couldn't do it anymore. He'd been there for twenty-three years and he'd had enough. So he rode out his sick leave and he retired. They don't let you accrue that much anymore, but that's the general idea. You save up your leave and you use it when you just can't stomach to look at the place.

A year into his sick leave, he promptly had a heart attack. That's why a lot of guys just don't retire. Or they retire, take a couple weeks off, and then they come back to work to start over. Some of the guys from the fed who had mandatory retirement didn't even wait until the ink dried on their last check before starting at the state prison. They didn't know anything else.

It was the same for my father. When my father had his heart attack, he drove himself to the hospital. That's the kind of man my father is. When he nailed his thumb to a board with a nail gun, he calmly inspected it, pulled the nail out, wrapped it with duct tape, and worked another eight hours. After his heart attack, what did he do? He got another job. My father is getting close to seventy now. He is blind in one eye, deaf in one ear, and still works full time. He still takes my kids running around hell's half acre for whatever hijinks they can talk him into. He takes my daughter to all of her riding lessons and shows. Half of the reason he still works is so that my daughter can take riding lessons, so she can participate in the shows, so she can do what she loves and build a foundation for the career she dreams of. And he's still got that thousand-yard stare that makes boys think twice about talking to my daughter. He taught me to drive; that alone is worth a medal of honor. This is the bar by which I measure all other men and why I find most of them lacking.

It is also the bar by which I measure myself, and I was not measuring up at all.

At this point in my life, I didn't think I ever could and it was a waste of time to try. I wanted him to be proud of me, but there was very little to admire in me then. I had a job and my kids had insurance. They didn't go to bed hungry, and that was the best I could say for myself. And even then, my parents were helping me by keeping my kids while I was at work.

I'd made a mess of things, but it was easier to think I had no other choice than to look at what I was doing.

day 112

THEY CALLED HIM COCOA PUFF.

    He was one of the biggest men I'd ever seen in my life. He was six foot something insane, had shoulders like pillars that could hold up a skyscraper, and he was round. I think he said once that he weighed something like four hundred pounds. He was also a queen, and I was very jealous of how well-groomed his eyebrows were. Still, it never got in the way of his job. Not his eyebrows, but his queen status. He wasn't too much of a lady to knock the shit out of some of these guys if they were froggy enough to jump.

    He came down to hear some of the disciplinary cases in Segregation, and it was always a good time when he was in the office. We always cut up in Seg, but it was even more of a good time when he came down.

    Although on this particular day, my arsenal of witty remarks was empty. I was fighting a losing battle with my bra, which wasn't really that unusual, but the underwire had broken through the seam and stabbed me in the armpit.

    It was hard to be the mistress of snark when I had a metal bar trying to work its way into my lung by way of my armpit. I had to do something. I waited until the whole crew was out on the tier, and then I reached into my shirt and I pulled that god-awful metal crescent of doom out of my bra. But just as I tugged it out of my shirt, Cocoa Puff came back in through the office door. I'd expected them to be out on the tier for a good long while, so the sight of him startled me and I pinched the ends too vigorously.

Said metal bit spun out of my hand and toward Cocoa Puff. His eyes widened and his mouth fell open as the thing barreled straight for him and pegged him squarely between the eyes.

I was already laughing so hard, I could have cried. And then he picked it up and examined it from all angles like it was some UFO dropped to earth.

"What is this?" he asked and then he put it on his head. Like a tiara.

If that wasn't enough, the First Sergeant came back through the door and snatched it off his head and put it on his own. They both did little dances around the office with my under-wire on their heads.

Finally, the First Sergeant asked again what it was, but I was engaged in laughter that was really more of a choking. I was finally able to wheeze out that it was part of my underwire for my bra.

Cocoa Puff blushed and said, "But it fit on my head."

The First Sergeant grinned and took it off his head and made a big show of measuring it against me from a distance and then putting it back on his head again. The thing achieved some kind of cult following, and as far as I know, it's still hidden somewhere in the Seg office.

See, it wasn't all brains and blood and death. There were times when we laughed, pranked, and built a cadre of moments that on the outside were nothing more complex than silliness. But it was those moments that bonded us together same as the darkness. They were like little glass globes we could pull out and look at with just a glance or a word between those who were there—frozen in time and a shining beacon that no matter how dark things got, those moments would come again.

day 113

ANOTHER SEG DAY, BRA MELTDOWN RESOLVED.
We were tearing shit up and taking names today. We got a tip from the investigations unit that someone had smuggled plugs of weed into Seg. Sure enough, we found them.

Plugs are exactly what they sound like. They're shaped about the length and breadth of three tampons if they'd been wrapped together, and they're transported in the prison wallet—anus. Or mangina, as it's sometimes called.

I was excited and called the Lieutenant to tell him we'd found them. He asked if I'd verified what was inside.

Uh oh.

I told him I hadn't and he told me I had to cut it open. So I got my multitool, I changed my gloves, and I sliced it open. I almost puked all over the table. It hadn't had a smell until I sliced it open. The stench that immediately filled the room was like we'd just crawled inside this guy's asshole—he'd had bad Mexican food for lunch.

Yes, and these guys roll this stuff up in porous rolling papers that smell just like ass and put it in their mouths. Inhale this smoke that has absorbed this man's ass like Vader and the dark side. That thought made me want to vomit all over again.

I wrapped it back up, documented my findings and sent it to

evidence, and wrote the disciplinary report. It took two days to get the office air back to tolerable.

day 120

IT WAS ONE OF THOSE DREADED "THREE WOMEN IN SEG" days. At least, dreaded for the rest of the institution. We liked our jobs.

That is, except for today. We'd gotten a guy in from the hospital who had gone out the week before in the care of EMS because he'd been shanked—sliced open like gutting the sickly white belly of a fish. He was running his mouth on us, and after dealing with him for five minutes, we all understood why he'd been shanked because we were ready to do it too.

The day he'd gotten shanked, he'd been a resident of the Medium and he'd been on his way back to his bunk for something, and this older convict had gotten in his way.

This older convict was the laundry porter. Well, the Medium didn't technically have a laundry porter, but it gave him something to do and made him feel useful. He was an old man doing the last of his hard forty, but he was respected, even by the young gangbangers, and the officers didn't mind that he wanted to work. He never got into any trouble; he was a convict, not an inmate.

The young, white inmate told him to hurry the fuck up and the old man didn't listen. He'd been doing time since before this guy was born, so he didn't pay him any mind. The cockbag pushed him and said, "I said get the fuck out of my way, nigger."

So the old man pulled himself to his feet and went on to the unit where he'd been headed to get the laundry carts. Instead of a laundry cart, though, he got a shank. He calmly found the guy who'd insulted him and ripped him open from belly to sternum.

When the guy came back, he looked like he'd had an industrial zipper implanted in his skin.

And he was still acting like an entitled cockbag.

Inmates don't get showers in the first forty-eight hours that they're in Seg. This bitch was crying about how he had to have a shower and he had to wash his stitches and we had violated his rights and he was going to sue us and…I don't even know what else he said because we stopped listening.

Then the Sergeant looked at me. She had The Look. The one she got on her face when she thought of something truly magnificent. She suggested that we give him a shower. And put him back in the showers with two of the biggest, angriest guys we could find who were scheduled to shower. It just so happened we chose a Crip and a Blood.

Yeah, buddy. Fuck you. That'll teach you to keep your racist shit to yourself and to shut the fuck up and do your time with your head down.

He should have known when all three of us came to get him for his shower, but no. He thought he was just getting his due. Which I guess he was. He had it coming.

Everything went smoothly until we went back to take them back to their cells, and one of the guys asked how he got those stitches. I wanted to raise my hand and say, "Pick me, pick me. I know!" He said it was a misunderstanding. Oh, I wanted to say something so badly, but that would have been endangering his life. He had enough rope; he could hang himself with it on his own.

If looks could really kill, the one he gave me would have

dropped me. He knew we'd put him in the showers with those other inmates specifically because he'd been spouting his racist crap and otherwise being more trouble than he was worth. I just shrugged. And the other two inmates both laughed, and one said, "Yeah, you push these bitches, they push back. I bet you're that guy the old man shanked 'cause you called him a nigger."

When loudmouth went back to his cell, we didn't hear anything out of him for the rest of the night.

I'm a big fan of inmates policing themselves.

day 123

I LEARNED THAT THE SERGEANT ON NIGHTS WAS FUCKING one of her corporals in the office upstairs. They found a used condom and she'd admitted to it.

I can say this for her: at least she wasn't inmate fucking. That was something.

But at work? Damn. Getting naughty in a prison isn't like other places. If you work in an office, you can get down in a supply closet, or the bathroom, or any number of places. When I worked for an airline, I had sex on the bag belt. And in the cockpit of a 747. So I understood the allure.

But it comes back to the fact this is a prison. Yes, we have supply closets and desks and bathrooms. But it's fucking prison. There's scabies, herpes, crabs, lice, shingles, Hepatitis Alphabet Soup, tuberculosis, fungi, meningitis, gonorrhea, MRSA, and HIV. Some of these things can live on surfaces and who knows what else. I wouldn't have been surprised to have found traces of the bubonic plague with all the roaches, rats, and vermin crawling around the place. And these people wanted to bear their soft mucous parts and expose them to all of this?

They weren't the only ones.

People used to fuck in the weight room until the administration installed cameras. In the yard bubble the windows are tinted, and the officer on duty in the bubble was caught jacking off while cruising the inmate database on the computer, talking to their pictures and calling them all sorts of naughty names.

The worst were the officers who got caught screwing the inmates. A girl I knew got fired for taking two inmates in the porter's closet and fucking them both. A food service worker was caught on tape doing two at a time in the kitchen and committing unholy acts with peanut butter. A male officer was caught on his knees in the library sucking off any inmate who'd pull down his pants. Incidentally, this service was advertised in graffiti in two of the cells in Seg.

A lot of what happened in the prison could be found recorded in graffiti. It's like a living history. Some of it was like a secret language that only the inmates knew. It was ever-evolving and ever-changing. As soon as we'd crack one code, they'd come up with something else. Most graffiti would be recorded and sent to investigations and then promptly painted over or destroyed.

It was frequently used to identify gang presence and members, contraband trafficking, and like the above-mentioned example, officers to watch because they'd stirred the pot and crossed a line.

day 140

MY MOM FINALLY HAD HER SURGERY.
Recovery didn't go well.

It took days for the anesthesia to wear off, for her to realize who she was and where she was. One time I went down to see her, she told me to leave because she didn't want to buy any Avon. Then another time, she asked if I'd seen her dog and talked about how much she loved living in Kenosha.

We were told there was a chance she wouldn't ever come out of the anesthesia.

I still didn't know if I'd have the chance to tell her I was sorry.

Part of me wanted to try to strike a deal with the universe, that if the powers that be would let her be okay, I'd forget all the other bullshit.

But I knew better than that. It didn't work that way. When I was in seventh grade, I sobbed on my knees praying every night to make my grandfather better when his kidneys shut down. I thought he was the only person in the world who understood me and I couldn't imagine a world without him. I didn't want to.

His shunts collapsed and the doctor refused to replace them, so he died.

I knew it didn't matter what I promised, or how good I said I'd be. If this was it, then this was it and there was nothing I could do about it.

day 141

I WAS IN THE MAX AGAIN. I USUALLY LOVED WORKING THE
Max, in Seg especially, but I could tell that today was going
to be one of those days.

It started when I realized I had nothing for lunch in the
fridge and no money to buy any groceries for two days. Yes,
way to be a responsible adult. I was late to work because some
asshole sideswiped my car and took off my mirror. I had to file
a police report so I'd have an excuse for not registering my car.
I still had to get it inspected, but it wouldn't pass without a side
mirror, and I couldn't register it without the inspection. And
after I got to work, I found a hole in my boot where the tread
had peeled away.

I collected my keys and equipment as quickly as possible so
the officer I relieved could be on her way. We were already locking up for Count so I headed down to the showers and flipped
the lights to let the guys know to finish up.

I gave them five minutes and flipped the lights again. This
asshole yells at me and says he'll be done when he's done. I
told him he had one minute before I turned off the water.
Count Time doesn't wait on inmates. Inmates wait on Count
Time. It happens at the same time every day and you know
when you have time to wash your ass. The whole institution
operates around Count Time—the set times every day when

each inmate had to be counted. Numbers were measured against rosters, which were measured again against a master list to double-check every one of our residents was where he was supposed to be.

He still hadn't come out a minute later and told me to fuck myself, to come in and get him.

So I turned off the water and I did go in and get him.

As soon as he saw my face inside the shower, he stormed naked to the OIC's office, dripping wet, and I followed behind him, ready to cuff him if I had to. The OIC told him they would talk after Count, preferably when he wasn't naked.

The inmate said he didn't give a fuck what I did or what I said because he'd get out the next day. I said that was fine, but I was still writing him a disciplinary report for interfering with Count and refusing a direct order. He could spend the last of his time in Seg.

After locking him up and performing Count, I finally had time to take note of a little motherfucker up on the second tier who kept running his suck every time I walked past. He'd say things like for me to move my fat ass on down his run, to not come back, to go fuck myself, etc. and so forth.

Finally, after handling most of my business, I stopped in front of his cell and leaned back against the railing. I was prepared to be camped out there for a while. He had to learn it wasn't his cell house, his tier, or even his cell. While I was in that cell house, that motherfucker belonged to me. He was just renting it and I would have respect from him, or at least a closed mouth for the rest of the night.

"What do you want, bitch?" he demanded, standing there, skinny and pale white in the neon of the overhead light.

I didn't answer him. I just stood there, staring. Inmates

walked past me going to work, going to callouts. Some stopped and talked. The ones who knew me just laughed and kept walking.

I stood there silently. When he couldn't get a rise out of me, couldn't get me to answer, he came unhinged. I almost wished I could have recorded it for posterity. He was zinging around his cell screaming at me like some possessed pinball.

When he finally started to settle down, I asked him if he was finished. He nodded. So I turned to walk away. Then I heard, "That's right, bitch. This is my tier."

So I came back to my perch. I'd drawn the line in the sand and I couldn't and wouldn't back down. It was a small thing, but it was something. I was going to have my way come hell, high water, or the Second Coming.

"Don't you have somewhere to be? Like the buffet?"

"I have lots of places to be. Right here is one of them."

"Aren't you tired of being insulted? Why don't you run along like a good little piggy?"

He was obviously trying to make me angry, but for me to be angry, I had to care what he thought of me. And I didn't. What I cared about was my reputation and how I was treated on the run. "Actually, I'm pretty tired of looking at your dumb freckled face, but you won't act like an adult so I can leave you alone. So, until you act like a grown-up, my ass is going to be parked right here." I pointed to the rails, where I'd sat down.

"You can't do that."

"I'm the officer. I have the keys. I can do whatever I want." I stayed there for another thirty minutes, the OIC seeing what I was doing and leaving me to it.

"If you stand in front of my cell, they'll think you're trying to get some of this." He pointed down at his body. He could have been built like one of the cover models for the romances I write, as quite a few of them were, and I still wouldn't have looked twice.

I laughed really hard. And loud. "No they won't. My OIC already knows what I'm doing and the inmates who know me know better. And you're about to know better too."

Although it was coming close to time to shit or get off the pot, so to speak. It was almost time for chow. I'd have to let him out. He was being aggressive, so technically, I didn't have to, but I didn't want it to escalate that far.

Finally, he said, "Sarge, I get the point."

"Do you?"

"Yes, ma'am."

"All I ask is that you treat me with respect and I'll give you the same, okay?"

"Yeah, I got it."

But he didn't get it. After chow, he refused to lock up. He said I wasn't such a badass when he was outside his cell. Of course, he said this all the way down the tier from me, but I'd learned a few tricks from some of the old-timers. So, rather than chase him all over hell's half acre, I went up to the second tier where his cell was and I had the OIC rack the door for me.

I went inside and shook the hell out of his house. He had a ton of nuisance contraband. Magazines that didn't have his name on them, extra pairs of state-issued whites like socks and underwear he wasn't supposed to have, an extra blanket, cleaning supplies that weren't allowed inside the cells except when the porters were passing cleaning materials. He had three indigent packs of grooming items even though he was only supposed to be issued one when he needed it. (They were for inmates who didn't have an industry job within the prison and had no family to put money on his accounts so they could buy things like soap, a toothbrush, or other necessities.) He also had an extra canteen bag that wasn't his. That was just the beginning.

So I yelled "yard sale" at the top of my lungs during the mass movement to chow and threw everything he wasn't allowed to have out of his cell down to the flag. He hadn't paid for any of it, at least not legally. It was all state-issued—or stolen—which I could take from him at will. The magazines I could have thrown away, which was essentially what I was doing.

Everything I threw down on the flag disappeared almost cartoonishly fast.

He charged up the stairs screaming at me, but when he got to his cell, he stopped. I half expected him to come in the cell and take a swing, but he didn't. Yeah, who was a badass only when he was locked up? This guy finally went into his cell cursing at me the whole way.

But I made my point.

Something he never let me forget. He held a grudge better than any woman I know. I ended up getting him down in Seg later, and we had another run-in. This one was a little more intense because he threw things at me and threatened to shank my "pink piggy ass." When I asked him why he was looking at my ass, he reached through the bars to choke me and jerk my head against them.

Rather than fight with him through the bars, I simply dropped to the floor and jerked his arms through, taking him with me. The momentum brought him crashing forward, smashing his face up against the bars like he'd tried to do to me.

Then it was really on.

So I followed procedure and told him he'd be losing his

privileges and going to a slam door cell and to turn around and face the wall with his wrists at the opening of the bean hole so I could cuff him. I knew he wouldn't comply. He was good and wound up by then.

Then he really lost his shit, so the other officer who'd seen the whole exchange went with me to tell the OIC and the OIC went back with me to try to get him to cuff up so we didn't have to call in the blacksuits and get them all dressed up in riot gear if this could be resolved at a lower level. But I knew it wouldn't be. This guy hated me.

I think because I made him feel powerless, but fuck him. This is prison. If being told what to do knots your knickers, don't go to prison. I'm not going to give him his way just so he can feel like a special snowflake. Treat them all the same.

And when he told my OIC to go fuck himself and to fuck me too, I couldn't stop smiling because I knew he was going to get his ass handed to him on a blacksuit platter.

"Are you sure?" I asked him like I would a kid who wanted to ride a roller coaster that I knew would be too intense for him.

"Fuck you."

"Really? Are you really, *really* sure? You can cuff up now."

"For you? Fuck you."

Okay, fuck me. Whatever. I wouldn't be the one going to sleep on a concrete slab in a paper dress with all of my mucous membranes burning like death.

I was firmly reprimanded with a smack to the back of the head when we got to the office. The Old Man said it was unprofessional that I would look so happy. I couldn't help it. This guy had been a huge pain in my ass. He obviously had something to prove.

Some of these blacksuit guys I hung out with outside of

work. We were drinking buddies. One even told God and everybody I was his little sister. He was black, so no one saw the resemblance, but I made sure to tell them that this inmate had said he was going to shank me.

They tried out the new pepper spray gel on him. Had a much better focus for the spray with gel rather than the aerosol. Better for the environment.

It burned hotter than the aerosol as well. This guy erupted in welts and blisters just from the spray. He still fought when we racked the door and the blacksuits went in on him to cuff him up and drag him out of the cell.

He must have been allergic to it because everywhere it touched him had swollen to twice its normal size. They had to walk him to the showers to rinse that shit off him or it would have just kept burning, and they passed by me.

The inmate tried to charge me, but I didn't move. If he'd have made it to me, I would have fucked him up, but I had complete faith in those guys and it wasn't misplaced. They launched themselves at him and buried his face in the concrete of the run to subdue him again before dragging him into the showers.

After that, he finally kept his mouth shut and his head down.

day 142

SEVERAL DAYS AGO, I'D FOUND AN INMATE PASSING A BOOK around from the Law Library. It hadn't been checked out to anyone in the cell house. I confiscated it and sent it back to the library. The inmate who'd been in possession of the book got very angry that I'd taken it. He told me I'd be sorry. So he riled up his little fangirl bitches who were on the block with him to find things to grieve me for. The first few weren't a big deal and didn't even make it past the first stage of complaint, meaning I didn't have to answer them. They wrote up their complaints and filed them with the administration, but they didn't make it past the Grievance Officer and were thrown out.

This grievance was different.

There was going to be questioning and, depending on my answers, possibly an investigation.

When I came into work, the relief OIC pulled me aside and kicked everyone out of the office before she sat me down and looked at me for a long time.

"What the fuck?" I knew she was about to lay something huge on me. This woman had no qualms about speaking her mind and suddenly she had to think about what she was saying? It couldn't be good.

"God, Sara." She sighed heavily. "I don't want to do this. But you should know, this happens to all of us. Especially those of us who are really good at our jobs." She shoved a paper at me and as I read, my knuckles whitened on the arm of the chair and if I could have shot fire from my eyes, I would have. It made me so nauseous, I promptly threw up. I scrambled to the bathroom and didn't even manage to close the door before I spewed my lunch.

Which was so noted by my commanding officer.

It was more disgusting than anything I'd come into contact with in the prison thus far. It was a horror far beyond swarms of roaches, rats the size of cats, and brain juice splattered all over me.

A knobby-kneed, buck-toothed, meth-faced, cock-sucking, illiterate motherfucker had accused me of approaching him for sex.

I didn't even know how to respond. I wondered if I could just puke on the page, scrape it into that little box where I was supposed to compose my answer, and send it back to him—hot and steamy with my disgust. Yes, this is my response to that. Have a nice day.

"Sara, you know they just did it to get under your skin and piss you off. Take some time before you respond. Then copy your response to all the brass so you're completely transparent on all of this."

I knew this guy belonged to the one who was angry with me over the book; he was one of his bitches. Literally. So I turned it off. I flipped the switch and detached myself from the situation and I reread the complaint. After I punched my fist into the wall a few times.

First, in his complaint he claimed I stopped by his cell multiple times the day previous. And I had gone by his cell, walked right past it, and I never stopped. Lucky for me it had been on camera. We'd been recording for the Force Cell Move with the guy who'd threatened to shank me, and never once did I stop at this inmate's cell.

Secondly, the things he claimed I said would never come out of my mouth in a million years. He said I asked to "conversate" with him. I hate that word more than explosive diarrhea. It's thug slang. You may converse. You may have a conversation, but you can't conversate because it's not a goddamn word. Thug is not my native language, although I will admit to using enough profanity to strip the hide off a trucker. Yet, even in my use of the profane, I do it correctly.

So I sat down to compose my response using as many fifty-dollar words as could be considered reasonable. I pointed out that I was on camera, his depictions of what was said, and how completely unlike my speech patterns they were, the incident about the book, and that I would never invite anyone into my body who didn't know the difference between "they're, their, and there."

A week later, I received a copy of the grievance back with all of my fifty-dollar words highlighted as well as a few others with the inmate's request to define them because he didn't understand my response.

Which was exactly what I intended. I made it clear the things he claimed I said were obviously not my words and I embarrassed him the way he embarrassed me. All of his buddies knew he'd filed the grievance and they would all want to see the response. So, not only was his grievance dismissed, but I made him look stupid to his friends as well.

He admitted later that he'd made it up, but in corrections, reputation is everything. Luckily, mine was solid enough with both inmates and staff to withstand this.

day 160

I LOVED MY JOB IN SEG, BUT I WANTED MORE. I NEEDED MORE money and I was ready for more responsibility. At work, anyway. A Sergeant position had come open and I'd filled out the sheet in human resources to interview for the promotion.

It consisted of a panel interview, so there were three people asking me questions, but I wasn't nervous because I knew all of the answers.

I knew I'd aced it when I got a call on shift right after my interview to ask me which of the Sergeant posts I wanted. Sometimes promotions involved a move to another shift, depending on how many slots were available. The applicant who scored the highest got first choice.

That was me!

I was elated that I'd been doing something right.

I chose a five-day open position rather than one where I knew I'd be assigned to a specific post every day. On the one hand, it sucked never knowing where I was going to be assigned from day to day, but also, if a post sucked, most likely I wouldn't be there again the next day. And being open would mean I'd get experience all over the institution and be available for more training and extra responsibilities so I could keep promoting.

Although, the higher up the ladder I promoted, the harder it would be to go to day shift. Day was a coveted shift because those people managed a semblance of a regular life. The waiting list to go to days could be long. It wouldn't necessarily be a schedule I count on either because every time I promoted, it was likely I'd get knocked back to second or third shift and back on a waiting list again.

But I didn't necessarily even want to go to days. Getting up at 4:00 a.m. does not a happy Amazon make. Day shift would mean more time with my kids, but I'd lose my shift differential, the extra pay I got for being on what was considered an "off shift."

Still, it was something to think about.

day 167

MY HUSBAND TOOK ME OUT TO LUNCH AT A NEW RESTAU-
rant in the city. He was proud of me and wanted to celebrate.

But this was not one of the good days. Things devolved into an ugly mess within minutes. I ended up throwing my plate at him, the waitress got in my face, and I told her she was going to get hers if she didn't get the fuck out of our business. Yeah, I was a real class act. I am now and forever banned from every location of this restaurant on the planet. I suppose I'm lucky I didn't go to jail.

The hard part for me was after stomping out of there, I still had to ride home with him. I wanted to disappear with my rage and chew on it for a while, but that would have meant walking home. Twenty-five miles.

Which, stubborn as I am, I seriously considered. In boots with three-inch heels.

I didn't actually *hit him* with the plate, by the way. He ducked.

Once we were in the car, he made me laugh, but that pissed me off even more because it didn't solve anything. Sure, I'd laughed, but I was still angry with him. Once I'd laughed, he always thought it was okay.

I told him I was still pissed and he said that I was always pissed. And he was right.

It shouldn't have been such a surprise, but it was. Now that I thought about it, I'd been pissed off for eight years. The whole time we'd been together. Why was I so angry?

Then he looked at me and said, "I know. When it hits you, it's really a surprise, but you keep thinking it shouldn't be." I just gaped at him and he continued. "Remember when you kicked me out of the house? You told me that I treated the inmates better than I did my own family. That stayed with me, you know. It sucked to realize it was true." Then he dropped another bomb on me.

"Anger is tied to expectation," he said.

Such a simple sentence, but it rang like a gong of truth. No, not pretty little bells, or some angelic choir of epiphany—a freaking gong. Loud, obnoxious, startling.

I realized that everything that had ever made me angry had been because I expected something different and maybe, just maybe, my expectations weren't reasonable. That was a nasty slap in the face. I had my first inkling that I expected more from everyone else than I did from myself—that I had a huge chip on my shoulder thinking the world owed me something.

It did owe me something, didn't it? After all the pain I'd already been through, all the sadness and heartbreak, why didn't it owe me some joy? It came back to me then, clear as the blue sky, what my friend had said about choosing to be happy.

We rode in silence the rest of the way home and we stopped at 7-Eleven for hot dogs since I'd spread our dinner all over the wall.

It was something to think about and I did think about it. A lot.

I didn't want to be angry anymore.

I used to be able to hold a grudge like no one else. I had no problem doing the proverbial slicing off my nose to spite my face. If crossed, I was something to fear. There was no amount of energy or resources I was unwilling to dedicate to the utter destruction of someone who'd crossed me.

But I realized something. I didn't want to be who I was.

But I hadn't quite gotten to the part where I realized I wanted to be happy. It seems like such a small step from realizing that you don't want to be unhappy to realizing that you want happiness. You'd think it would be a given, but it wasn't.

Happiness and unhappiness are active choices. We can choose to be happy. Things happen, we can't control everything, but we can control how we react to them. On a logical level, I knew that. But it hadn't clicked yet that I was choosing to be miserable.

day 168

I WORKED IN THE MEDIUM AS A CORPORAL BECAUSE WE were overstaffed on Sergeants, and the body alarms started malfunctioning. Body alarms, the buttons we carried and pushed when there was an emergency and we needed the cavalry, demand no small amount of exertion. Ten alarms sounded before five o'clock that evening, and we had to respond to each alarm and treat it as an emergency regardless of whether we thought it was false. Our legs felt like mint jelly from all the running.

The communications guy tried to fix the malfunction, and we thought he had it locked and cocked, finally. That's why everyone hauled ass with both hands when the emergency tones for another alarm came over the radio during open yard time after chow. The Control officer announced that the alarm was in the clinic.

The yard officer I was running with dropped her radio.

We couldn't leave it lying there because we didn't want an inmate to get hold of it, making him privy to private operational communications, nor did we want to make an officer wait if someone was really in trouble. I mistakenly thought I could bend over and scoop it up as I ran.

I bent over, but instead of rising up out of the bend, I skidded across the cement of the track on the yard in front of more than three hundred inmates. I think they heard the laughter on Mars.

Hurt like a motherfucker, I skinned the palms of my hands, my knees, and my cheek. I flipped them all the bird and got up and continued responding to the alarm. It was called false just as I went flying through the clinic door.

The Lieutenant thought I'd been fighting on the way. I had to tell her it was just a battle with my fat ass not wanting to do what I told it. We had a laugh and I was headed back to my post when the nurse on duty took one look at my face and hauled me back into the business part of the clinic by my ear. She insisted on cleaning up all my cuts and slathering them in Bactine. I didn't complain. I didn't fancy walking around that festering hole with open sores on my body.

Later, the Lieutenant offered to put a note of commendation in my file because I'd fallen and hurt myself but continued responding. I declined, but thanked her for the offer. I didn't consider a skinned knee hurting myself. Stabbed in the face maybe. I just did my job. It wasn't above or beyond the call of duty.

The call of duty was to get to the officer who may be in trouble and render whatever aid necessary. I did that. Period. I did just what I would want someone to do if they were responding to my alarm.

day 169

I'D BEEN A SERGEANT FOR EXACTLY THREE DAYS AND I'D YET to run my own cell house, meaning I'd yet to be in charge of other staff and oversee the operations. One hour into the shift on this night, a First Sergeant had to go home for a family emergency. The Captain called me to ask if I thought I could run his house.

I'd be working out of class, working a position that was a rank above mine, in what they called the animal house. Three tiers of assholes known for starting fires, throwing flaming rolls of toilet paper, and, most recently, pegging an officer in the back of the head with a soup because they didn't like the way she enforced policy.

Hell yeah, I could do it.

As soon as I took over for the OIC, there were a flood of inmates trying to talk to me, following me around as I went about my duties, or spilling into the office either to see what kind of Sergeant I was or trying to get me to approve something the regular OIC wouldn't have.

It was impossible for me to get an accountability count done, so I locked them down. No rec time, no phone, no library, no nothing until I had accurate and verified numbers of where all my inmates were.

They didn't like this much, but there were no flaming rolls of toilet paper, no mattress fires. No one threw anything at me as I passed each cell or when I was walking on the tiers.

Why? I'd made use of the porters—inmate workers who saw to the upkeep of the cell house, oversaw the distribution and accounting of cleaning supplies, linens, etc.

Back in the old days of corrections, porters ran the prisons. They were in charge of the tiers and when shit needed to be handled, they handled it. It wasn't so much like that anymore, but they were still a useful tool when you wanted to distribute information.

They would come into the office and try to look over your shoulder, spreading whatever business you were doing all around the cell house. If you were writing a disciplinary report, if you were about to search someone's cell, whatever bit of information they could gather.

I talked to the head porter first thing. He came up and introduced himself, asked me if I needed anything, and asked me questions about myself. All things he would carry back to the tier. As well as whatever he thought they'd be able to get past me.

So, I obliged him. I told him things I wanted all the inmates to know. Like what would happen to them if they started fires and "sparked" while I was running the house. Sparking is when they would use things like paperclips to get a spark from their electrical outlets. They'd use that to start fires if they didn't have any lighters or matches hidden somewhere. It would also short out the breaker and send the whole cell house into darkness.

I figured if they had enough toilet paper to light on fire, they didn't need more. They knew that sparking shorted out the circuits, so obviously they must want to sit in the dark. So, if they wanted to be stuck in their cells wiping their asses with their hands in the dark, that was no skin off my ass. And if they hit me with something they'd thrown? God help them because no one else would be able to.

The porter was laughing so hard by this point, he almost couldn't speak to ask me what exactly it was I would do if I got hit with whatever they were throwing, be it urine, feces, or spunk. They were known to throw all three.

I told him that as a woman, I had ammunition more horrible than anything they could ever dream up. And whoever hit me may not feel my vengeance today, tomorrow, or even in a year. But it would happen and if I got fired, I didn't care. I could go get another job, but the guy who hit me with something would forever be the guy who got slapped in the face with a used tampon. No matter where he went, no matter how much time he did, no matter what else he ever did with his life, that story would live on forever.

He was horrified.

And so were all the other inmates in the house.

Granted, they still tried to get away with shit, but when I caught them or called them on it, no one had anything nasty to say and there were no projectiles, flaming or otherwise, in the cell house that night.

day 170

I WAS ASSIGNED TO THAT SAME CELL HOUSE THE NEXT DAY. The schedule of movement for inmates was crazy, but I managed. On my shift, inmates might be out of their cells for many different reasons, ranging from religious services, going to chow, library privileges, recreation time on the yard, showering—and all of that had to be monitored and checked, to ensure that everyone was going where they were supposed to be.

It's hard for any officer working in a new cell house to monitor everyone, since you don't know faces yet, and it's imperative that inmates who aren't engaging in sanctioned activities be locked back in their cells. Otherwise, contraband can be passed, and other possibly dangerous activities can occur. The two regular officers who were assigned there were fantastic. It was a great team effort.

But it would have been too easy for the night to go off without something happening.

Around six p.m., my phone rang and it was one of the new officers on shift—straight out of training. She was crying, sobbing like someone had run over her dog. I told her to call the Captain's office and get someone to relieve her and tell the Captain she needed to come to my cell house.

I'd told all the new officers out of training to call me if they ever had any problems and they were unsure about what to do. I didn't claim to know everything, but I knew I could point them in the right direction. Even if it was just going with them to talk to the Captain. In training they told us that when we excluded new officers from the pack and made them feel they had more in common with the inmates than other officers, that's when they were prime prey for the inmates to turn dirty. So making myself available to rookies for questions or whatever they needed was me doing my part to try to make the institution a safer place.

On her first day of OJT, I told this officer who had called me that she needed to wear less makeup. Yes, if you like makeup, you should wear it. And in an ideal world, you wouldn't be treated differently because you wear makeup. But this wasn't an ideal world. It's fucking prison. If you come in painted like a French whore, that's a signal to them you're looking for a man and you will be targeted. Period.

Personal rights are all well and good, but be aware of your environment. Inmates don't care about other's rights. Obviously.

Anyway, she came in to my office still bawling. I locked the office door and just hugged her and let her cry for a little bit. Then I got her to tell me what had her so upset. She'd been running the chapel—overseeing the religious gatherings—and three inmates had cornered her, telling her they knew where they could go where the camera wouldn't see them. They'd put their hands on her ass, her breasts, between her legs.

My first question was why she hadn't called an alarm. With three against one, even I would have hit the button that signaled my body alarm and brought the cavalry running, and I'd been known to follow an inmate down the tier in a rage after he'd grabbed me and demand "what the fuck" rather than push my body alarm.

She said she was too afraid.

But that's the point of the alarm. If you're ever in fear for your life, hit that button. Any situation you can't handle alone, hit that button. If she'd hit that button, the fury of all hell would have been unleashed on those poor bastards, with ten to fifteen officers responding, trained like Pavlov's fucking dogs to fight when they hear that alarm.

That training was a part of what made watching my husband car shopping such a treat. At most dealerships, they have a tone that plays over the intercom to let a salesman know there is a phone call or a customer on the floor. These tones they use sound exactly like the tones that sounded over the radio at the prison when an alarm was called. Every time they went off, he launched himself from the chair and looked a bit like a rabid dog. I wouldn't want fifteen of him ready to knock me on my ass.

Anyway, because she didn't call the alarm, she lost credibility with both officers and inmates. Inmates had no respect for dirty officers even though they tried constantly to turn them. They knew as a dirty officer she wouldn't be fair, firm, or consistent. The officers had already been wary of her because she wore such heavy makeup, but this was the last nail in her coffin. The only officers who would talk to her after that were others who were suspected of being dirty.

It was generally believed that she didn't call the alarm because she invited the contact. That she changed her mind later after she realized how much shit she could be in.

This belief was only solidified when she got caught having a relationship with an inmate. I wasn't surprised. I just knew she wouldn't last. She set off my Dirty Bitch Detector and I knew it was only a matter of time before they turned her.

She had low self-esteem. The inmates look for that, a chink

in the armor—somewhere they can burrow in and get inside your head.

I have a copy of an inmate instruction guide called "How to Have an Inappropriate Relationship with Staff," which they've passed amongst themselves. The title in itself is funny because that's what they call it in the staff training: inappropriate relationships with staff.

Someone has written special instructions for what to look for in an officer who's prime to be turned and how to prime them if they aren't.

The first thing on the list is someone who obviously has low self-esteem. Someone who doesn't often make eye contact, who doesn't hold their head up. It's like culling the sick gazelle from the rest of the herd.

The next step is to talk to the officer, and while it happens with men too, it's usually women who are targeted. Talk to her every day, ask her how she is and be sympathetic. Listen to everything she says. Be aware of her moods and react accordingly. Offer her something she doesn't get at home.

Then do something so she knows she's special to you. Make yourself stand out. Be patient. Promise her you can keep a secret. Establish that your relationship is different than what she has with anyone else, staff or inmate.

It goes on from there, step by step, and those tactics have worked countless times. Officers have sacrificed careers and family, even endangered lives in the community.

One woman, not an officer but a volunteer with a program inside the prison, was turned by a convicted murderer who was twenty-one years younger than she was. She had a family, a husband and children, and she walked away from them to be with this man. She gave him a gun and helped him escape, smuggling him out in one of the program's vehicles. When she was interviewed by a local paper after her trial, the first thing they quoted was that she said this inmate was someone she could really talk to.

day 190

THE PRELIMINARY TESTS AFTER MY MOTHER'S SURGERY showed that they got the entire tumor and that she was cancer free. That was good news, but we began to suspect that she had a stroke on the table or some other catastrophic event. She was having auditory and visual hallucinations. She was convinced that things were happening around her that weren't. And she'd get very angry when told that she was mistaken.

She kept having episodes in which it was like she'd short-circuit and get stuck in a certain position, or she'd fall. She went back to the doctor who'd performed her surgery and when she did fall, the doctor sneered at her and told her she was fine and to get up. The doctor didn't offer my mother any assistance, or even any compassion. *The doctor saw a woman fall—a woman who had come to her about post-surgical issues involving this very thing—and the doctor insisted she was fine without even examining her.*

What a cunt. I don't use that word very often; it's an icky word and, for most women, a fighting word. I say it here with relish. If I ever see this woman again, this word will sit on my tongue like the finest artisan chocolate and will taste even sweeter when I spit it at her.

I wish I'd have been there because I would have taken a bite out of this bitch so large, she'd still be looking for the rest of her ass with both hands. When people are sick, they are more easily managed, especially by someone they see as an authority figure who knows more than they do. They just want to know that someone is going to make them feel better. When you go to a caregiver, the treatment my mother got is not the kind of treatment one would, or should, expect. The doctor thought she could treat my mother that way because she was sick and aging.

And my mother thinks the sun rises and sets on those initials after the doctor's name, so she'd never argue with one, even to defend herself against a wrong as obvious as this one. She hasn't learned to be an advocate for her own health yet.

I've learned to let go of a lot of things now, but this wasn't one of them. I hope someday this doctor is sick and terrified. That her body betrays her and someone treats her the same way she treated my mother.

She also double billed for several visits. Now that, I could do something about. I have a certificate in medical billing and coding, so I called the office and got that handled right away. I also turned the incident in to the insurance commissioner so she'd most likely get an audit. After all, if the bitch had done that to my mother for more than one visit, how many other sick people was she double billing and taking advantage of?

I also finally took the opportunity to tell my mother that I was sorry. I got emotional and choked up, so it didn't come out the way I wanted it to. I didn't say everything I wanted to say. How much I still needed her to be my mom. How I was sorry that when she first got sick, I didn't notice. I didn't help her. How I was too caught up in my own shit to think about her. All I said was that I was sorry about everything and that I loved her.

I know now I'm really lucky that I got a chance to say that. I'd let so many things go unsaid. Unrecognized. It was another bright, burning banner for all that I didn't like about my life.

And myself.

I'd been directing all of my disgust outward for so long that when I finally looked inside, it was a mess of nuclear proportions. The light was too bright, and while I'd managed to own up to what I'd done wrong with my mother, I wasn't ready to look at the rest of it. That sort of introspection required a bottle of bourbon so I could forget it all in the morning.

day 197

I WORKED A FIRST SERGEANT POST AGAIN, ONE STEP ABOVE
my current rank. That was an awesome feeling.

I was still in the Max, which also made me happy. Until I
saw who one of my officers was going to be. This guy was nice
to me, but he was dumber than a box of hair. He also stuffed his
pants with a sock.

When asked about it, he swore it was some kind of tumor
or gigantism of the balls, but on intense observation, a sock
was all it could be. I've never known a man who could lean his
junk against a table and have the table move said junk down to
his knee and he not make some sort of high-pitched sound. Or
stop breathing.

He didn't know how to talk to people, or really how to do
his job at all. He would have been tolerable had he been open
to learning or hearing what another more experienced officer
had to say, but he wasn't. He was convinced he was smarter than
everyone else.

I'd worked with him before, one time in Seg. It wasn't a good
experience. You know when you're coming up the stairs and you
hear an inmate say, "Don't do it, it's Sarge," that someone is in
for a world of shit. Literally. That time I had peeked up over the
railing in Seg and the inmate who'd been speaking smiled at me.
"You're good," he'd said.

I asked him what had them wound up enough to throw things. When this officer had passed out chow, he'd refused to pass the other things that went around with chow. Grievance forms, toilet paper, other request forms, etc. Chow times were the only times these inmates had to get these things. But regardless of that, they had them coming. You give them what they have coming. No more. No less. And they were entitled to these things.

I told them I would take care of it.

That was something else. Do what you say you're going to. Period. I told them I would handle it and they believed me. I also told them as fun as I'm sure it would be to tag him in the face with a shit bomb, he was still an officer and I couldn't let them treat an officer that way.

I talked to this officer and the first thing out of his mouth was, "Fuck 'em." No. Not fuck 'em. Do your fucking job. Outside of that, sure. Then he said he couldn't go back up on the tier because he was afraid of getting hit with whatever they were going to throw.

Too bad.

He made his bed and whether it was shit or roses, I wasn't cleaning it up.

Although I did watch him from the bottom tier as he made his rounds, and the inmates noticed this. I'm sure if I hadn't been there, he would have gotten a shit gun to the face.

So needless to say, I wasn't looking forward to working with him again. He'd cost me three hours of my night in Seg when all the inmates were locked up. I could only imagine the night I was going to have with them out and running around and him shooting his mouth off.

I wasn't disappointed.

First of all, he caught an inmate—a kitchen worker—trying to sneak produce back to his cell. So he confiscated it. Okay, he did something right. No, that was too much to hope for. He ate the pepper he took after I told him not to, and then mid-bite the Lieutenant came in for a post check. Looked bad for him and for me. I got my ass reamed because I didn't stop him. What was I supposed to do, jerk it out of his mouth and get into a scuffle with another officer in full view of the inmates over food? Yeah, I'd never live that down.

Then, after the Lieutenant had left and I was already butt sore, an inmate walked by the officer's station, and this officer made a snide remark to the inmate. It was obvious from the look on the inmate's face that they didn't have the kind of rapport that engendered that sort of thing, so I waited for the inmate to pass and then I corrected him. I would never correct a fellow officer in front of an inmate.

The officer laughed, grabbed the mic, and made an announcement to the entire cell house, calling the inmate by name and telling him to go straight to his cell and not to stop and suck his boyfriend's cock on the way.

I kind of want to bang my head on my desk just remembering this fuckery. Like so many other acts of wanton stupidity, you have to remember where you are. This is prison, not the eighth grade party where you kissed the girl who sat in front of you in math and then tied her bra to the ceiling fan.

Everyone has cred to maintain in prison. Yes, this inmate was gay. Yes, his boyfriend lived in the same cell house. Everyone knew it, but to call it out like that over the intercom was disrespectful. This officer should have been prepared to take whatever consequences he had coming. Dishing out crap and then hiding behind the uniform was a sure way to get yourself shanked.

Five minutes later, almost time for Count, and this officer was up on his tier. Suddenly I heard an alarm come over the radio. An alarm from *my* cell house.

Motherfucker.

There was one other officer up on the third tier, but I knew it wasn't him. It was dumbass on tier two. I charged up the stairs as fast as I could, adrenaline racing, running through a thousand scenarios in my head and what I would do—only to find him standing there with his thumb up his ass and the inmate he'd been harassing standing in front of his cell, refusing to go inside.

Before I had the chance to handle the situation, first responders filled the tier, headed up by the same Captain I'd had to explain my womanly needs to. He was ready to kill someone. He filled the width of the tier, his legs were braced apart, and he reminded me of a bull getting ready to charge. For one horrible moment, I really thought I'd see smoke come out of his nostrils and he'd leave me as a sad little ink stain on the floor.

But I found my balls and asked what was going on.

"He refused to lock up," the officer said.

"Did he threaten you?"

"No."

This shit did not require an alarm. "Why didn't you call me?"

"He refused a direct order."

The Captain deflated slowly but was still obviously pissed.

"Go to the office. Right now."

"But—"

"Go!" I turned to the inmate. "Are you going to lock up?"

"No problem, Sarge." He went into his cell.

As we were walking back down to the office, the Captain took me aside and asked me what I knew of the situation. I told him about the events leading up to what had happened. All he said was, "Counsel your corporal."

I so desperately wanted to say he wasn't *my* corporal. But that's not a team mentality. I was supposed to be in charge of shit and I couldn't handle the corporal in my cell house. "Most definitely."

"Then send him to me for further counseling and write something to put in his file about the counseling and the incident."

day 198

SAME CELL HOUSE THE NEXT DAY.

And they sent me another dipshit.

I started to understand why corrections officers have such a bad reputation. This guy looked just like Milton from *Office Space*. Dead ringer. He stared at me blankly for the first few minutes of the shift. My mouth moved, words were coming out, but he didn't assimilate any of it.

I told him to get out on the tier and start locking up for first Count. Instead, he sat down at the desk right next to me.

First of all, I like my personal space. I don't have a personal bubble; I have a personal brick. All the better to smack people who invade said personal area. But that wasn't the most horrific part. The part that had me almost ripping off my own skin was that his arms were covered in sores. Not just little mosquito-like bites he might have scratched, but full-on oozing, leprosy-looking, ulcerated, open-wound sores. Like infected spider bites.

The hallmarks of MRSA.

MRSA is a dirty bastard of an infection. Its technical name is *Methicillin-resistant Staphylococcus aureus*. Which means it's resistant to antibiotics. It can also live on surfaces for months at a time.

And he'd rubbed his arm on mine.

"So, what's that on your arm?" I asked, trying not scream and light him on fire.

"Spider bites."

"Wow, you must have a lot of spiders."

"I guess so. I think they were in the barn I cleaned out yesterday."

"You think?"

"Yeah, I just woke up and had it."

Oh, the fuck you did.

"You know," I said as I drenched my arm in hand sanitizer, "prison is dirty. There's all sorts of things living on the surfaces here. It's not a good place to have open wounds. If that's not MRSA, you could get it. Or anything else that could infect you through an open wound. Hepatitis, HIV, if someone who is infected gets hurt. You need to have that looked at."

"Yeah, I will tomorrow," he said and went to the staff bathroom before I could say anything else.

Tomorrow? The fuck you say.

An inmate knocked on the office door. "Uh, I don't mean any disrespect, but you have to get that man out of here. Is that MRSA on his arm?" His voice hit a note higher than anything I could hit. He was bordering on the edge of freaking out too.

"I don't know what it is, but we've got a handle on it."

I did have to get him out of there. That shit on his arm wasn't healthy for anyone. Especially not me because I was going to freak right the fuck out. Yeah, I could handle a man's brains on me, but this guy's creeping crud twisted my guts.

When he came back, I sent him to the Captain's office and they sent him to the clinic. He returned to the cell house with his arms bandaged from the wrist to the elbow.

A few days later he called me to thank me for making him get it looked at. It was MRSA.

This man did not belong in a corrections environment. This incident was a banner for every reason why. He wasn't aware of his surroundings and couldn't think farther ahead than his next meal.

The next time I had to work with him, an alarm called in another cell house, and his position in our cell house meant he was a first responder. Officers were running out of their cell houses as if the hounds of hell slavered at their heels and "Milton" wandered up to me casually and told me he couldn't respond to the alarm because he had a heart condition and that I needed to go.

Lives depend on first responders. He was not someone I would trust to guard my back. I was more than happy to call the Captain and get him the hell out of my cell house.

day 217

IT'S AMAZING HOW ONE PERSON CAN HAVE A CERTAIN RAPPORT with someone and another person's interactions can be completely the opposite.

For example, there was one inmate I didn't particularly like, but he seemed to want to talk to me every second he could be near me. I didn't have to look up his crime to know he was a sex offender. When I first came on shift, he would always try to stand too close and he would lick his lips incessantly when talking to me, making this sound like he was eye-fucking some scrumptious bit of cake.

I told him I found it offensive, and if he wanted to speak to me, he would do it without sucking on his lips or making that sound. A couple of the other officers I had talked to about it told me not to say anything, to just let it go. That he'd do it more if he knew it bothered me. But I'm not one to keep my mouth shut if I find something unacceptable. I had done nothing but treat him with respect, and I expected the same.

He actually apologized and told me that it was meant as a compliment. Um, no. He was a misogynist who thought all women were whores who could be manipulated or cowed into submission. He did like that I was willing to speak with him, though, so he did it on my terms.

I even ended up talking to him about how he treated another

officer, a friend of mine. He made her cry by saying all sorts of nasty things about her weight. He said even being without a woman as he had for ten years, he still wouldn't fuck her, etc., and so on. First, I gave her shit that she let him see how upset he'd made her. He was a sex offender. With them, it's all about the power they can have over you. I told him I was disappointed in him for treating her with such disrespect. He'd said she didn't deserve respect because she didn't stand up and take it.

She told me he gave her the "heebie jeebies"—she'd looked up his crime and she didn't even want him breathing the same air she did. She wouldn't look him in the eye because she didn't want to look at him at all. But being a predator, he took that as fear and zeroed in on her.

Same guy, two officers, completely different result.

While that's no surprise, because no two people will have the same experience with one another, inmates and officers assume they will get similar treatment from people they know are connected. Officers will expect inmates who are related to behave a certain way—good or bad depending on how their relation behaves since they come from the same circumstances. And inmates will expect officers who are related to behave similarly.

When the two officers were my husband and I, inmates always commented on the differences between us.

I knew I'd made it as an officer when my husband came to second shift for a while when he promoted to Sergeant. When the inmates sent the porter to talk to him to see what kind of officer he was, what his expectations were, the inmate told him that the cell house didn't have to be like Seg.

My husband was confused and said he didn't know what the inmate was talking about. The inmate responded that he'd heard something about a real hard-ass named Lunsford who had just come out of Segregation and that it didn't have to be like that, that they could all "just get along." My husband laughed and said, "You're talking about my wife." The inmate didn't quite know what to do with that.

But I did. I went out to celebrate that night. I wasn't just a bitch, or a whore, or a cunt. I wasn't female. I was an officer. I was a hard-ass. Consistently. Firmly. Hopefully fairly. I was simply authority. That meant something.

While we were on the same shift (we never worked the same cell house or even the same security level), I was asked a hundred times if "the other Lunsford" was my husband. Most of the time, I just wanted to raise my eyebrow and scowl. Lunsford, like Sasek, wasn't like Smith. It's kind of unique. At least in parts of the country where my father-in-law didn't live for very long.

When I would acknowledge the question, I'd never get a neutral response. It was either, "Wow, that guy is a bastard. How do you stand it?" "No wonder he's such a dick being married to you." Or even "Poor guy. What did he do to deserve you?" But eventually, after dealing with us both on a long-term basis, a few inmates decided, and loudly I might add, that we deserved each other.

I'd been gone for a year when my husband went into work one night with pot roast. An inmate asked him if I'd made it for him and my husband responded that I had. The inmate clicked his tongue and shook his head and told him he should employ a food taster because he wouldn't trust anything I'd made. I was the most evil woman ever to walk the earth.

I still laugh when my husband tells that story. I don't think I was ever evil. I may have had to whip my dick out a few times, but they had it coming. My dad always said to give them what they had coming.

Then there were other guys who I had absolutely no problem with who took major issue with my husband. One got out and threatened him on camera at a gas station. Said he was going to come to our house, rape and kill me and our children. My husband filed a police report, so that way if he did come to the house and we riddled him with bullets, we'd have the paperwork to back us up. But the next we heard of him, he'd beaten his girlfriend's four-year-old son to death.

And when he was in my cell house, I'd never heard a peep out of him.

day 229

My OLDEST DAUGHTER GOT AN INVITATION TO A BIRTHDAY party. It was for the son of one of the women who'd been inmate fucking. The one who'd invested her life savings to get this pedophile out of prison. She wanted him, the one with the rotten dick, to come live with her and her passel of kids.

My daughter really liked this boy as a person. Said he was super nice. But with a mother who made choices like that, I could only imagine the other things this kid had been through. Not only that, but a good officer will not associate with you after you cross a line like that. As I said before, it's not always about the truth of a situation, but how it appears. Socializing outside of work with someone with that reputation, well, it doesn't look good.

So I told my daughter she couldn't go and I told her that if the little boy asks why to tell him that she already had something she had to do. While I'm a big proponent of telling the truth, I didn't see any reason to hurt this child over something his mother had done or put my kid in that position.

At one point, the officer had signed up to be the room mom for my other child's class. I sent a letter to the school board detailing her documented association with a pedophile.

And I know this sucks for my kids, not being able to have certain friends because of how it could affect their parents' (now just their father's) career. I hope they understand when they're older that if these people could negatively impact their father's career, then they're not the type of people who are going to be good for them in the long run.

I remember when I was a child and we lived on prison prop- erty, a small community of tiny little cottages sat across the street. There were always lots of kids over there, but the street was very busy. I always wanted to go over there and play. I'd been invited so many times. I was allowed to walk to the gas station that was right next to the cottages, and sometimes the kids would walk over too and get candy.

But I wasn't supposed to talk to them. That housing was for inmate families who were relocating or here on an extended visit.

I thought it was a stupid rule at the time, but I understand now.

day 230–238

I HAD NO ASSIGNED POST ON THE SCHEDULE. ON THIS DAY I ended up in the cell house that had become my husband's regular post. When I got there, the atmosphere crackled with another strange mix of respect, fear, and outright dislike. I hadn't worked this cell house before, so I knew the feeling was a blend of residual from my husband and the reputation I'd earned.

While I was a stickler for the rules, as long as everyone was doing what they were supposed to be doing, I was laid-back and easy to deal with. The inmates in this cell house didn't call me Lunsford, Sarge, CO—only Mrs. Lunsford. Even the ones who didn't like me.

This cell house had special rules—it was an open honor dorm for private industry workers, and the inmates weren't forced in their cells very often. They could be out in common rooms watching TV or using the microwave, and they even had a washer and dryer so their clothes didn't necessarily have to go out to the laundry. That was a huge perk because for some reason, the laundry had bigger roaches than the kitchen.

It was here in this cell house I learned to make a new kind of dessert. One day I smelled the most divine thing coming from the microwave. I went to investigate and I saw an inmate pull this cake out of the microwave. I know they didn't sell cake mix in the canteen, but these guys were crafty. They had scraped the inside crème out of Hydrox cookies and mashed the outside cookies into a fine powder. Then they added half a can of Sprite before baking it for two minutes in the microwave. They frosted it with the leftover crème from the middle. My porter gave me the recipe and I did actually try it at home, and it turned out pretty well. Almost tasted as good as it smelled.

My porter was an interesting guy. He was helpful without being overly so. Funny without being grasping or desperate for attention. When he did talk to me, it was never anything deeper than what was appropriate. He kept mostly to himself and stayed out of trouble. On the surface. I did notice he was very well respected by the other inmates, but I thought it was because he was a convict, not an inmate. He'd done a lot of time and still had a lot more to do. He'd never see his family again outside the prison walls, but he didn't let that mold who he was. He was calm and had a healthy respect for the old-school way of doing things, as did I.

The regular Sergeant for this house on my shift ended up taking some leave, so I worked the post quite a bit. I got to know the guys there fairly well.

On one really quiet night, when everything was winding down, this porter asked me to use the phone. It wasn't technically his night, but he was a good porter and everyone who'd wanted to use the phone had gotten their chance. A simple request, one I could approve or deny a hundred times a day. Really, of very little consequence to me. As a porter, he was allowed to have these extra little things if the OIC approved. Which I did. Turned out it was his ailing mother's birthday. She didn't have many birthdays left; in fact, he was sure this would be her last one.

I didn't know any of that. He didn't try to use that information to get me to feel sorry for him or manipulate me to get his way. He just approached me and asked like a grown man. I guess you could say I respected him.

I tried to treat all of the guys with respect, but that didn't mean I actually respected them. I did have respect for most of the convicts who did their time like men rather than like needy little bitches who thought the world owed them something. I tended to pay attention when those who acted like men said things to me because most of them didn't talk just to hear their gums flap.

I worked in another cell house again before I was back in this one. When I'd been in the other cell house, a guy had flashed me. He'd been standing at the bars with his dick out, but dressed in all of his winter gear. Hat, coat, gloves, dick flailing out of his jeans in the breeze. I'd laughed, but I'd still written him up. When he'd been served with the write-up, he came down to the office and cussed me out in Spanish. I recognized crazy whore, bitch, and something about fucking my mother.

Back in the first cell house, I related this story to my second officer. My porter happened to be there listening. His whole face turned red and he asked me who had done this to me. I told him it wasn't important. I wasn't going to reveal that information. Then he asked if it was one of his people. I didn't know how to answer that. His people? Inmates? Mexicans? What? I didn't know what he meant. Well, yeah, it had been a Mexican, but I wasn't sure if that's what he was asking, and I didn't want to offend him. So I asked him if he meant a Mexican, or an inmate, or what. He said in a very measured tone, "Mexican." And I said I didn't know his nationality for certain, but he was obviously of Latin descent.

I'd actually never seen him that angry. He wasn't demonstrative, but you know, sometimes it's the quiet ones you have to watch out for.

The next day I got a written apology in Spanish and English from the inmate who'd done it. He pled guilty to the write-up and didn't even contest it. When I saw him again, he apologized in person. Gone were the accusations of crazy bitch whore, replaced with Señora Lunsford.

That was when I discovered my porter was the head of a certain Mexican gang for all of the Midwest territory.

For the rest of my employment there, I never had anyone of Latin descent treat me with anything other than kid gloves.

Once, when I was working overtime and standing chow (supervising the inmates while they got their meal trays and ate), an inmate got nasty with me in front of a group of Mexican inmates. I was just going to take his badge number and write him a disciplinary report. It wasn't a big deal to me. But it was strongly suggested that he get out of line and go back to his cell. He checked into PC, or Protective Custody, later that day. The Mexicans told him if he spoke to me like that again, they'd rip out his tongue and replace it with his dick.

All because I let one man make a phone call.

day 250

A WOMAN FROM WORK INVITED ME OUT WITH HER, AND I agreed. She was support staff, not an officer, but I'd seen her in a few of the places I went to regularly. Plus, my regular crew of drinking buddies was having a hard time keeping up with me and I didn't want to go out alone.

She said she knew a bar where we could drink for free because her boyfriend's family owned it. Her boyfriend was barely twenty, but she was older than me, mid-forties. I appreciated her style—free was definitely good. Even with friends paying for some of my drinks, I'd been spending way too much money.

It was a country bar, but they played hip-hop sometimes too. A strange combination to see guys in cowboy hats, boots, and with enormous belt buckles dancing to Kanye West. We co-opted a corner and she introduced me to a bunch of her friends, including the stripper who was paying her rent.

I was immediately accepted into the group and treated as if I'd always been a part of it. So much so that when they started laughing and joking about things that had happened nights previous, some of them would swear on their mother's graves I'd been there with them.

That was nice in a sense. It felt like being accepted unconditionally. That's a good feeling, even though it was obviously a mirage. These people didn't really know me, and I didn't know them. They never would really know me because I'd learned I had to keep myself at a distance.

I'd only had one pitcher of Coors when my stomach revolted and I almost puked all over the bar. As soon as it welled in my throat, I launched myself toward the bathrooms. The entrance had no door and the individual stalls had saloon doors. I flung open the first set of doors and my cheeks billowed out, full of beer-puke…

And there was some poor woman with her knickers around her ankles, her knees locked together and eyes as wide as twin moons in her heart-shaped face.

I managed to hold off just in time to rear back and then barrel through the next set of doors where I redecorated the entire stall. It spewed from my mouth with no effort at all, and it was like trying to aim a fire hose. It wouldn't stop coming. I tried my damnedest to get it into the toilet, but there was too much inertia.

The woman in the other stall finished her business and came over and held my hair and even helped me clean it up. Yeah, I can be a bitch, but I'm not an asshole. I made the mess so I tried to clean it up. Especially since we were drinking for free.

I never saw that woman again, but she must have been some kind of saint to help a stranger clean up projectile vomit in a bar bathroom. Especially since I'd almost puked all over her.

This is another point where I should have seen what I was doing to myself. I should have realized for as much as I valued control, I had none over myself.

But I didn't. Instead, I staggered out of the bathroom after rinsing out the rags and decided that I should probably stick to the hard liquor. I drank and danced until closing time.

The group decided to go back to my friend's house to continue the party, and she drove. I didn't realize she was as drunk as I was until she crashed the car into the ditch about a mile from her house.

We stumbled out of the car and walked the rest of the way.

We were still having a good time, but the party started to wind down around four and that was when she put me in a really awkward position.

She called me back to her bedroom and closed the door. She asked if I wanted to go to another party, pulling a baggie out of her purse that had a little white thing in it that looked like a rock. It was cocaine.

I was pretty far gone on the downward spiral, but I wouldn't take that step. Something in me just knew that I wouldn't come back.

So I told her that wasn't my thing and I left.

Then I had to decide if I was going to write a report and turn it in to the investigations unit. She was my friend and I wasn't a rat. I believed in the blue wall. But I also knew that if she was doing cocaine, it wouldn't be long until she was bringing the shit inside the walls to pay to feed her addiction. That's the nature of the beast.

In the end, I didn't feel I had any choice. She wasn't just hurting herself. She could get people I cared about hurt. Maybe even killed. So I turned her in.

I felt this horrible weight in my stomach with every stroke of the pen as I wrote out my narrative about what had happened, but I did it.

Turned out to be the right thing to do. It wasn't long before she was caught having a relationship with an inmate and allowed to resign. They never caught her with drugs on her, but they knew she was bringing them in.

day 262

MY HUSBAND ASKED ME TO GO OUT FOR LUNCH AND THEN to Best Buy for some media shopping.

I wasn't sure; I didn't want to be banned for life from Best Buy, too. Whenever we were in the same room, we fought, and part of why I'd left him was because I didn't have the energy to fight with him anymore. It had gotten to where I lost myself, and I'd been a pale shadow of the woman I used to be. His words had the power to slice me deeper than any blade—to dig into my marrow. He's the only person who I really cared about what he thought of me.

So to avoid that pain, I'd stopped being me. I'd stopped fighting because I just couldn't stand it anymore. Before we separated, there were days I'd wake up and count the minutes until I could go to sleep again because that meant I'd hashed another day off. I wondered when it would be over. After leaving him, the person I turned into was no better.

But I could never resist him. He's the most charismatic person I've ever known, and the draw between us is like the tide. You can't fight it; all you can do is go where it takes you. Even when you dig your feet in, it gnaws away at the ground beneath your feet until suddenly you're waist deep when you'd only wanted to get your toes wet.

When we first separated, he'd come over one night to get the kids and he'd backed me up against the wall like a quarterback would a cheerleader under the bleachers and there were butterflies in my stomach just like when we'd first met. He kissed me then and I swear to God there was an orchestra.

Just like our first kiss.

They were both everything a romance novel kiss is supposed to be. I'd never experienced that before him, and I thought they didn't happen. But they do. I could have drowned in him.

And my husband, for all of his talents, is a master manipulator. He could con the Devil into church. So it was on the tip of my tongue to say I didn't want to go, but I found myself saying yes instead.

We had a leisurely lunch and we strolled around Best Buy, poking at this and that. One of my favorite things to do is browse appliances and dream about what my house is going to be like when I finally have one of my own.

Etta James's "*At Last*" came over the speakers and he motioned for me to come over to the CD section, so I did. He grabbed me around the waist and slow danced with me in the middle of Best Buy. Everyone was looking at us, but we didn't care. It was only him and me.

When the song ended, he kissed my forehead and went back to browsing as if it had been an everyday occurrence.

day 279

I'VE ALREADY SAID THAT SEARCHING CELLS IS SOMETHING I like to do. Except in the Minimum unit. Those guys owned way too much stuff, and the area I had to search wasn't cells per se. It was a dorm there, a large open space called a pod with twenty-plus beds to a pod, and four pods to a unit. Each inmate had a locker, and guys were always meandering around. It wasn't safe to have your head buried in someone's property all the time because you wouldn't always be aware of your surroundings.

A favorite technique of one of the Sergeants I knew was to make an announcement throughout the dorm and say that the blacksuits were on their way up to shake down the house. If they had anything they wanted to get rid of, to do it and then he'd go behind the cell house, gather it all up, and it would be out of the dorm. Of course, sometimes, he'd actually have to get the blacksuits to show up once in a while or the threat lost its bite.

I was doing it the old-fashioned way and going through their lockers. I found a cup, which in and of itself wasn't a big deal. They're all allowed to have cups. It's what was in it. The cup could hold approximately twenty-two ounces and it was packed to the rim with semen.

Yes. *Semen.*

Dirty motherfuckers.

Sweet fucking hell but I was glad I had on gloves. I called the clinic for a bio-waste bag. I guess I could have dumped it in the toilet, but then what? It was against regulations to keep bodily excretions. No, I'd rather just give it to people who deal with that kind of thing. Namely someone who wasn't me.

And what the hell was he going to do with it? Throw it on someone? It looked like it had been there for a long time—the edges were crusty and there was some kind of crisp rag standing in it, saluting me.

Working the prison almost put me off men completely. Seeing all those dicks in my face every day, always being on my guard because someone always wanted something from me, seeing what kind of animals people could be…The inmates were always fond of saying if you treat a man like an animal and put him in a cage, he'll become an animal. But I think that's a cop-out. You choose your actions. You choose the words that come out of your mouth, and it's messages from your brain that causes your muscles to move your hands, your feet, your body. You choose to be an animal.

And the filth. Dear God, the filth. Pissing on their cells, themselves, throwing their own feces like monkeys in the zoo, and trying to cover everything that would stand still with semen. I'm supposed to have empathy for them? It's a hard to thing to remember that the man trying to coat you in his shit is someone's son, someone's brother, someone's universe. As officers, we're faced with that choice too, the choice to be an animal or a decent human being. Officers get institutionalized too. Again, that's why they say the first year you're no good for The Job and after that you're no good for anything else.

It's also said that a society's prison system is how best to measure their civilization. If that's so, we're fucked.

day 282

I WENT TO A FRIEND'S HOUSE FOR A BRUNCH, AND I WAS reminded why I don't socialize with people outside of those I know from work. Sure, part of it isn't intentional—that isolation—but some of it is. There are some opinions I have that are based on my life experience, not some idea or philosophy that blossoms from a do-gooder who doesn't know what they're talking about, regardless of the degrees on their wall.

Someone all of us knew was arrested for molesting four kids. Invariably, the conversation turned to pedophiles, their treatments, and how to "fix" them.

They can't be fixed.

"Studies show..." I spaced out as soon as I heard this. Blah fucking blah. I work with them every day. I don't want to hear a bunch of crap about what their professors told them in school or what they think they learned in practicals.

You want to call them fixed and let them out? Fine. Let them live in your neighborhood. Oh, what? No? You wouldn't want a pedophile or a rapist for a neighbor? But haven't they completed their programs? Aren't they "fixed"?

So I was sitting there nursing a mimosa and thinking about how fast I could get out of there without offending my friend. The rest of the women I could give a shit about, but this woman had been my friend for a long time.

She saw on my face that I was uncomfortable, and she tried to steer the conversation to something else, but the rest of her guests were determined. I got up to take my plate and my drink to the kitchen and duck out.

I didn't want to turn my friend's nice brunch into a pissing match by talking shop. The whole point of getting out of the house and hanging with her was so I didn't have to talk shop.

"Sara, you work with them. What do you think?" one of them asked.

Why? Why did she have to ask me? I just wanted to relax, and I didn't want to discuss anything more serious than what kind of champagne was in the mimosa.

"I think treatment makes them more efficient predators." It leapt out of my mouth before I could stop myself.

"How else are they going to get better?" This woman looked at me, shocked.

There was nothing for it now but to explain what I meant. I knew she would stop listening as soon as I got to a point she disagreed with. Her question was really to enforce what she said rather than an actual query.

"They're not going to. Pedophiles and sex offenders can't be fixed."

She laughed and lifted her nose in the air. "Well, maybe we should save this discussion for when *you* have a degree, hmm?"

"Or when *you* work with them in a real-life setting instead of in your office where they kiss your ass because the court says they have to see you and they know what they tell you affects their probation and freedom? Right. Like I said before, you think you can fix them? Let them hang out with your kid. How much faith do you have in your fix?" I said.

"They just need someone to understand them. Most of them were molested as children themselves."

I give not a fuck. Sure, I'm sorry for any child's suffering, but that doesn't excuse their actions. They make their own choices. "You know, you sound like those women who fangirl serial killers. *He just needs a woman who understands him.* You think you can fix them too and you can't. Some behaviors, once they're hardwired, that's it." It's more about managing the ideation and self-control rather than a fix.

"Well, that's true but—"

"But what? I work with them while they're getting these programs that are supposed to help them blend in to society. To fit with the rest of us. And that's what they do, but it's not fixing what's inside them. The programs teach them the behaviors they need to slip among us unnoticed. They make them more effective predators."

She looked horrified. "I never thought of it that way."

I continued. "Just the other day I was searching a guy's cell. He'd been through his mandated programs, and he had a picture he'd cut out of a Christian pamphlet about finding a family with God. It was a picture of a little girl and her mother. He'd taped it up by the head of his bunk. There was just something about it that struck me as off. Maybe you might have thought that he was using that as a focal point to get him through his dark times, that it was something to look forward to, a family. But I took it. I could have given it back if it was appropriate for him to have it, so I went to check to see if he was a sex offender. And you know what, he was."

The psychiatrist put her hand over her eyes, as if that would block out whatever images had cropped up in her head. She knew what he'd been using that picture for. I did too. He'd been jerking off to it.

"He asked me later if I'd taken it. I said I had. Most inmates, when you take something from them, even if they're not supposed to have it, raise hell. Instead, he asked me quietly if I'd taken it because it was inappropriate, or because it was *inappropriate for him*. He knew I knew. I didn't even answer, I just looked at him and he said he understood."

"Oh God!" One of the other guests just caught on to my meaning.

"There was another one—he'd completed his programs and was due for release in two weeks. When I was searching his cell, I found a cardboard tube taped underneath the drawer of his desk. It was decorated with glitter, happy faces, and hearts. On the inside was a newspaper clipping from one of the local schools and it had pictures of kids reading and playing. Each one was labeled meticulously with words like pussy-bearer and fuckhole."

"Did he get out?" one of the other women asked.

"Well, yeah." I shrugged. "He did his time. He completed his programs. He's out now."

Then they all looked at our psychiatrist friend like it was her fault he was out, not the judge who'd handed down his sentence. Then everyone wanted more stories from the prison.

"You should write this stuff down," my friend said. "You obviously have an audience."

Everyone who works corrections thinks at one time or another they should write it down.

I thought about it. At least then I wouldn't have to repeat myself. Some of the stories are fun to tell and then others, like this one, these are the things I wish I could forget. Then again, sometimes I'm glad I can't forget them because I know what to look for and I can better protect my family.

The old adage about not judging a book by its cover? Absolute crap, at least when it comes to people. None of us are perfect, but there are some flaws that are markers, big red warning signs to the rest of the herd that there's a wolf under that wool.

In nature, it's called aposematism. Loosely defined, it's how nature marks creatures as poisonous. The violin on the brown recluse spider, the bright red of the poison frog, and the brightly colored coral snake—they all signify that these creatures are poisonous and deadly.

To me, it shows up in symmetry. None of us are perfect, so no one's features are going to be perfectly symmetrical, but I noticed the most violent offenders are all asymmetrical. If you look at pictures of some of the more well-known serial killers, their features are misaligned, and the most common trait among them is large ears with one hanging obviously lower than the other. (Again, that's not to say that just because one of your neighbor's ears is longer than the other that he's got his wife's head in his freezer.) And to be clear, aposematism as it applies to people is just my observation and opinion; it hasn't been studied scientifically. Although I think it would make an interesting study, and I plan to pursue it while working toward my degree in clinical psych.

In my experience, there are traits specific to every deviance. The most notable were the child molesters. It's easy to believe that every white male over forty who is in a prison setting is a child molester, but that's not the case. There is a certain softness about such sex offenders that's evident around their eyes and their mouths, something that marks them for what they are, a faux innocence.

In fact, whatever their deviance, the eyes are the best marker. It's not always something that shows up in pictures, but it can. There is a certain flat emptiness to the eyes of a sociopath, and no matter how congenial or how charming, that never changes. The best description is like looking into a mirror and getting the distinct impression that what's looking back at you isn't you, it's nothing like you, but a monster pretending to wear your face.

I do judge people by how they look because my gut is rarely wrong. We used to play a game with the inmate database called Ugly Thug Ball. We'd email each other the pictures of some of the ugliest inmates we could find, but it morphed into something else. We'd try to guess an inmate's crime just from his picture. I was right around 95 percent of the time.

A friend of mine had started dating through an online dating site, and she sent me pictures of her dates to get my opinion. One guy looked normal and healthy. Average. There was nothing exceptionally remarkable about him, but there was something about his eyes. I immediately asked her how much time he'd done. She said a couple of years. I asked her if it was for drugs and she said yes and laughed. She thought it was amazing that I just knew.

day 300

MY OLDEST DAUGHTER AND I GOT INTO A NASTY FIGHT. I don't remember how it started, but it ended with her saying that she didn't want to be my daughter. So I told her I didn't want to be her mother either, and I took her back to my parents' house and dropped her off. I told them I'd give them the money my husband was giving me for her care—I was done with her.

I know as a mother, I'm supposed to be above that. Kids say shitty things, they're ungrateful. They're supposed to be. They're kids.

But I was still very much a kid too.

Fuck, but I'd failed at everything.

I began to think that I should have given her up for adoption when she was born, not because I really didn't want to be her mother, but because I was no good at it. She didn't want me to be her mother.

And with good reason. I was a failure.

Just like I knew I would be. I'd let my mother convince me that I could do this, be a mom. She told me I was a fuck-up enough times that she should have known better too.

When I found out I was pregnant, I'd called a friend of mine and told her my library book was late. She asked if I thought I had a fine and I said I wasn't sure. So I went to her house where I took six tests. They were all positive.

So I went to the doctor to be sure, and when I got the call, I didn't know what to do, but my mother was there watching me and she just knew. She said, "You're pregnant."

The idea of abortion never entered my mind. I would never tell anyone else not to have one, or what choices to make for their bodies, but I wouldn't have one. Adoption was an option though. I'm adopted myself and I know that I and my biological mother both had so many more opportunities because of her choice. I wanted to make sure that I made the right choice for this child and for me.

I never wanted children. I didn't want to get married; I didn't want any kind of commitment on my time. I didn't know how to be a mother. I was too selfish.

Yet there I was. I realized I was right not to want those things because I couldn't do them. A failed marriage, failed motherhood, failed everything.

I was still failing at being a daughter. My mother had just come through cancer and I was dumping my kid on her because I couldn't handle my responsibilities.

I emailed my friend in Portland after it happened. She said everything would circle back in time. That I'd get through this. My daughter would get through this. That our family would get through this one way or another.

And she was right. She's always right.

As I'm writing this, my oldest daughter is sitting across from me at the breakfast bar. Just looking at her, I have a profound sense of joy that the universe gave her to me. I almost fucked it up. I'm thankful I didn't and for how well-adjusted she really is. I have this overwhelming urge to jump up and down and spike a football, screaming, "I didn't break her!"

I really thought the hospital staff was insane for handing

her to me after she was born. They just shoved her in my arms with a diaper and a smile like it would all be okay. They give you a 230-some-page booklet with a Blu-ray player and with a kid, this whole other person, nothing but instructions for how to take care of her bellybutton. What about the rest of it? Sheer madness.

"Momma, what's wrong?" I love that she's fourteen now and she still calls me Momma.

"Nothing. Just working on the memoir."

"Aww. I love you." She comes and hugs me. She wants to read it, but I won't let her. There is so much in this book I hope she never has to know. I'm sure when she's older she'll snag a copy somewhere.

That was a huge part of the decision about whether I should write this book. I never want her to blame herself for things that happen later. Either of my girls. I made my choices myself. But I decided it was important to share everything that happened to me if I could help someone else make it through.

I hug her back. "If you need me," she says, "I can listen. You know I get that from you."

Sometimes, I think her heart is big enough to love the whole world. With all my screw-ups, I wonder what I did to deserve her. Or my other daughter, who is just as wonderful and beautiful and just as loving.

I don't want to think that maybe I was their trial, their cross to bear, but if I was, and this was the worst they ever had to live through, then maybe I did something right after all.

I can see that now, how lucky I am that all of my selfishness and immaturity didn't maim them in some way. Back then all I could see was me.

day 303

YOU KNOW THE STAGE OF DRUNK WHERE YOU FEEL THE
need to tell everyone how drunk you are? It's not cute and
everyone just nods in agreement, but really, they just want you
to shut up. Unless they're as drunk as you are and then you can
laugh about it and take turns telling each other how drunk you
are. "Oh my god, dude. I'm so fucking drunk." And for some
reason, that's the funniest damn thing you've ever heard in your
life. So funny, you fall over. But you're too drunk to sit back up.

Yeah, I'd passed that ten rum and pineapples ago.

I was so drunk it felt like my stomach had said, "Fuck you,
I'm out," and got up and walked away without me. But I wasn't
ready to be done, not yet. The world was a horrible fucking
place and I needed some tequila rose-tinted glasses to even
look at the motherfucker.

My stripper friend who kept buying me drinks on some
guy's credit card was crying in her beer, but with good reason.
She'd just found out that a good friend of hers had been the
previously unidentified, charred body they'd found outside
some ghetto club in the city. She'd been having trouble with
a stalker and he'd caught her after work, opened up her veins,
and lit her on fire.

This woman died screaming in an alleyway next to a dumpster and was discarded like so much trash.

She was someone's child. Someone had rocked her to sleep, made sure her cake had chocolate frosting on her birthday, and firmly closed her closet door to keep the monsters inside.

And for every story like hers, there were hundreds more. For every horror that we hear about, as soon as we turn the page there's another victim, another life, another river of blood on the pavement, and we look and nod and say that's really fucking sad, but we go on about our business, ever thankful that it didn't happen to us.

Some guy slid in the seat next to me at our table. I looked at him. He obviously wanted something. He pushed a beer at me, but it was already opened. Even drunk off my ass I know better than to take an open consumable from someone I don't know.

He shrugged, as if to say: your loss. "Hey, so my bro over there?" He pointed across the bar. "That big, badass-looking motherfucker? Yeah. He thinks you're hot."

I looked around the bar, and I was sure that maybe I was drunker than I originally thought because the only big guy on that side of the room was a guy who'd just gotten out of prison. He was huge, about six-foot-five, which was normally my type if he hadn't been an inmate, but badass? I almost snorted my beer. He'd been in Pussy Control. Better known as PC, or Protective Custody. There are no badasses in PC. Take your lumps and stop sucking down eight balls you can't pay for. Someone's threatened to hurt you? It's prison. Man the fuck up. Or cry like a little girl who lost her ice cream and go to Pussy Control.

"I'm not his type." I tried to go back to what I was doing—which was consoling my friend and pickling my own liver the hard way.

"A big bitch like you? You're just his type." He looked me up and down. "And he just got out of prison."

"First, I said no. End of fucking story. Like you're slick enough to talk me into fucking him, and the fact he just got out of prison—a place crawling with MRSA, HIV, and hepatitis—that's supposed to make him attractive to me? Really? And second, can you not see my friend is upset? So, even if I were so inclined, which I'm not, I'm kind of busy."

"Fucking cunt," he growled and slapped over a bowl of peanuts as he stood.

"Is that what your boyfriend calls you when you're sucking his dick?" I stood up as I spoke.

He stepped closer to me and for one second, I thought he was going to hit me. And I wanted him to. I wanted him to hit me because all the rage I had—layer after layer built up inside of me—it was like a dam, and that crash of his knuckles into my face was all I needed to let that wall crumble. In those seconds, time stopped. I had exactly four things within my immediate reach I could use as weapons to defend myself: a pool stick, my drink glass, the chair, or the table. My buzz was gone; I didn't feel drunk anymore, just ready to fight. He was a male. (I won't say a man.) So what? I was bigger and I knew I hit harder. Plus he was an asshole. In my mind, the perfect target for me to vent all of my pent-up rage. I was fairly giddy with the idea of that kind of release.

He didn't say anything, just stared at me and took another step closer. As if that would intimidate me. We were only inches apart, and all he had to do was lay one little finger on me, and I'd break it and shove it up his ass. I was spoiling to fight.

"I asked you a question, cocksucker." I wasn't going to be the one to throw the first punch because I had my job to worry about, but neither would I take his shit or back down.

Everyone in the bar stopped what they were doing and

looked at us. Or at least that's what it felt like. The bouncers were watching, but they hadn't acted. I think they wanted to see what would happen.

Suddenly, the big guy was there too with his hand between his friend and me. "Hey, I'm sorry, he just—" And he broke off mid-sentence when he saw my face up close. "Oh, fuck. Sarge, I didn't know it was you. You look different out of uniform."

He looked at me, and there was a certain plea on his face. He nodded for his friend to leave. I'm sure he didn't want to get in trouble. He hadn't maxed out his time and he was out on parole. So he probably shouldn't have been in the bar to start with, but I wasn't there to bust his balls. He had a parole officer for that.

"Fuck that fat bitch," his friend said and shoved his way over to the door.

"He's not doing you any favors, man," I said to the former inmate.

"Yeah, I know." He looked at his feet. "But you do look pretty tonight, Lunsford."

My first thought was that only a guy who just got out of prison would think I looked good by that point in the night. Or a guy who was still trying to get his dick wet. I was drunk, my hair was wrecked from dancing, I was sweaty, and I was sure my eyeliner had run down my face, making me look like a raccoon on meth. But he picked up the bowl his friend had knocked over and put it back up on the table and turned to leave.

Sometimes, when they get out, those guys just wanted to be acknowledged as men instead of numbers. Especially by us, the officers. It's a little thing, just a nod or a word, but it goes a long way to how they see themselves. It's not thug-hugging, it's just human decency. And I guess I had a little of that left.

"Hey," I called out and he turned. "Thanks." I took another

drink. "And good luck. I don't want to see your face in my house anymore, okay?"

"No, ma'am. I won't be coming back."

"Good to hear."

"Take care of yourself, Lunsford."

"Yeah, you too."

He left and I dunked my face back into the sweet oblivion of my rum and pineapple. It didn't take long for the buzz to come back or my stomach to revolt again. By two o'clock, my vision wasn't just blurry, I almost couldn't see. My head felt like it was spinning around on my shoulders like Regan from *The Exorcist*, and thoughts were coming to me half-formed. All I wanted was to be home so I could close my eyes.

By this point in the night, I'd had two pitchers of Coors and seventeen rum and pineapples.

I don't think I told my friend I was leaving. I just wandered out of the bar and walked home. I'm lucky I made it. There was a small bridge I had to cross over and a spindly little creek below. I'm sure if I'd passed out and fallen, or just tripped and fell over the edge, I would have split my head open on the rocks below. I probably would have looked a lot like that guy I saw on the yard who'd had a lock in a sock taken to his head—rotten watermelon and sausage spread out all over the little creek.

After staggering in the front door, I finally caught up with my gut. Remember, it had walked away from me earlier. It slammed back into me with the force of a wrecking ball and up out of my throat. I barely made it to the bathtub.

It flew in a liquid projectile missile out of my mouth, and even having a solid count of the drinks, I didn't realize how much alcohol I'd actually ingested until the bottom of the tub was coated with orange vomit. I choked and it shot out of my nose. I couldn't breathe, my eyes were watering, and there was snot and liquor running down my face. My stomach heaved and convulsed, propelling everything that was inside out. I puked so hard the force of it burst a blood vessel in my eye and hot piss running down my leg, pooling on the tile beneath me.

In that moment, I was suddenly outside my body looking down at my own head bent over the bathtub, puke in my hair, and piss on the floor—the absolute fucking train wreck I'd made of myself.

There was a song that had become my anthem for a while. It was called "Thrash Unreal" by Against Me! and it played in my head over and over. That's when I realized it wasn't an anthem; it was an excuse. It was a crutch—it was a big tampon because I was being a giant pussy. (Sorry, Against Me! You rock. It's not your fault I used your song to plug it up like a tampon.)

Disgust bloomed bright and hot in my head and some of the lyrics came to me then too: "*No mother ever thinks that their daughter will grow up to be a junkie, no mother ever dreams that her daughter will grow up to sleep alone.*" No one ever dreams they'll grow up to be a boozed-out, bar-whore corrections officer with no future and no dreams either. And that's exactly what I was. If I saw someone else doing this to themselves, I would have had no pity, no sympathy. Fuck you, you're doing it yourself. You have nothing to complain about. Pull up your fucking pants and do what has to be done. This is *your* fault, you sloppy bitch.

And it was. Yes, cue the music and the light from above as the epiphany hit me with a brick. This was all my own doing. Yes, the world was in fact a horrible place, but I was making it worse all on my own.

My kids deserved better.

I deserved better.

I'd had dreams once. That was the whole point in leaving my husband. We didn't make each other happy. More than that, we were toxic to each other. But this wasn't any better. I still despised myself.

I hadn't been any warrior woman. I wasn't worthy of the Morrigan's mark I'd put on my body. In prison gangs, if you mark yourself with one of their tattoos that you haven't earned, they give you the option of removing it yourself any way you can, or they remove it for you. Usually by removing the skin with the offending tat. I didn't deserve the raven watching my back. I hadn't managed my hearth or my war. I hadn't found me; I was even more lost than I had been before.

And not that I thought that some avenging Irish raven goddess was going to swoop down out of the sky and peck her mark off my skin, but it was the embodiment of the strengths I'd thought I possessed and the ones I wanted to call my own.

I decided in that moment I would make my life what I wanted.

And I passed out on my bathroom floor.

I AWOKE THE NEXT DAY WITH A HANGOVER FROM HELL. Of course, it was nothing less than what I deserved for being such a sloppy bitch and doing so many horrible things to my body. My head thumped like a freight train running on nitro, my stomach was sour, and my tongue was like a llama hide that had been left on the floor of a taxi cab.

Every bone in my body ached. There were places on me that hurt that I didn't even know had nerve endings. My muscles hurt—my stomach from puking, my arms from holding me aloft over the sea of orange puke, my legs from—hell, I didn't know. My hip and ribs were sore from sleeping all night on the ceramic tiled floor of the bathroom.

The stench of alcohol, curdled orange juice, and urine turned my stomach again, but thankfully, there was nothing left in my belly to purge.

I remembered everything so clearly, especially that moment where I was outside my body. I half-wished I could do that again because being inside hurt like a bitch.

But I guessed it would hurt for a while—until I straightened myself out. There would be no hanging out away from myself; I had to find a way to be comfortable in my own skin. If I didn't like who I was, I had to change it.

I peeled off my clothes, still disgusted with myself. I got

the Comet and a Brillo pad to scour the tub, which was a feat of ridiculous proportions considering how hung over I was, but with every thrust of the pad against that orange ring, I got another flash of determination.

This would not be my life.

I would not be this person.

I scrubbed that tub until it gleamed. The smell of the Comet played as much hell with my stomach as the other offending scents. I was thankful to rinse it away and replace it all with the clean tang of Pine Sol when I mopped the floor.

I felt slightly crazy mopping my floor naked, but it seemed like something that had to happen. I couldn't stand the filth for another second. Not the filth I'd brought into my home, spewed in my tub, or dribbled on the floor. It all had to go.

I got into the shower and proceeded to scrub the filth from the previous night from my body. There was something therapeutic in that, almost like I could wash everything away with the dirt.

Then I had to scrub my tub again.

It felt good to be clean.

I was scared that the rest of it wouldn't be so easy because I wasn't quite sure how far down the rabbit hole I'd fallen.

Was I an alcoholic? Would I be able to stop by myself? I steeled myself for that eventuality, that I would need help. Would I get sick when I didn't drink? Would I get the shakes?

Then I shut all those questions down because it didn't matter what the answer was to any of them because I was going to do it. I was done using the bottle to self-medicate. Whatever it took to change what I'd done to myself, I'd do.

And if it sucked sweaty donkey balls, well, that was just tough shit. That was the price I'd have to pay to get my life back on track.

day 320

I REALLY THOUGHT IT WOULD BE HARDER TO STOP DRINKING to get drunk. My psychiatrist friend told me that I was lucky I didn't have an addictive personality or it would be something I'd have to fight the rest of my life. It was great she had so much confidence me because I didn't. Not yet. I wasn't naïve enough to think I could just decide to stop. I didn't even know if I was an alcoholic.

That sounds stupid, but I didn't. Was I addicted? My behavior sure seemed to indicate so.

And yet I did stop. Cold turkey.

The first week, I was tempted. Who wouldn't need a drink after looking at the fuck-all mess I'd made of my life? But I knew that wouldn't fix anything. Understanding I wasn't an alcoholic made it worse. If I was an alcoholic, I'd have a reason. Not that it would excuse my behavior, but a medical condition was more forgivable than wanton fuckery.

I didn't go out with friends at first because I didn't trust myself. Over the course of several months, I found I could go out with friends and not drink, but I didn't want to go out with most of them because they weren't conducive to the changes I wanted to make in my life either. They were just as bad as the alcohol, all in the same place I'd been in: miserable and self-medicating with nothing to look forward to but more of the same. So I made different friends.

I still went out for the occasional game of pool, but those invites began to taper off and I was okay with that. They stopped calling me and I stopped calling them.

I wasn't lonely in that same way I'd been before. There wasn't the same empty chasm I was trying to fill with the drinking and the partying. I was still sad and alone, but I could see some daylight.

It was years before I had another drop of alcohol, before I could be sure that I was the one in charge. Sometimes I drink socially now, and I joke about how many glasses of wine I've had or how much it will take to get me to do karaoke (and believe me, no one wants that), but I always know where my line is and I never cross it because I will never be that person again. I will never choose to be numb no matter what life throws at me.

When I made that choice, decided that I would never choose to be numb, I still hadn't figured out that when I made those lines in the sand that Fate or the Universe, God, whatever, would test me. That's what those lines are for; they're ultimatums of a sort, a big, fat dare to the powers that be.

The darkest part was still to come.

day 321

PRISON WAS STILL PRISON. NOTHING CHANGED THERE.

That big blowup we'd been expecting never happened, but sometimes, that's just how it is.

I started thinking about school and maybe going back for a criminal justice degree. Or abnormal psychology. I had a brain, and when it wasn't soaked in rum, it liked to be busy. I didn't think about a journalism degree—that seemed too close to reaching for the stars, and I'd barely crawled out of the dark. I needed a safe dream that I knew I could reach for and obtain because I wouldn't stop with the degree. I'd get ideas in my head and try to write books. Books that had one chance in a million of selling. I wasn't ready to handle rejection yet, especially not something that was so personal, a piece of me.

Unless it was from the inmates. I still didn't give a shit about that.

We had another new class of officers coming in, as with the high turnover rate there were new classes of trainees every few months. I never minded having them in my cell house for OJT, or On the Job Training. They had to learn sometime, and I knew a lot of officers didn't have the patience. The thinking was that they didn't know if these people were going to stay, so why invest in them?

At the fed, you're lower than dog shit until you've done your first year. No matter where you came from, whom you're related to, the other officers don't want to hear anything out of your mouth until you've done your year. I could see the logic in that. At the state level, there was no particular time limit. Some people were never trusted, and others were trusted immediately.

But I was determined that incoming classes would learn more on OJT than I did. For a lot of the officers, especially the old-timers, training consisted of handing them the keys and showing them where the lockbox was with a quick, "Don't get shanked and I'll see you in eight hours."

My first bout of employment with the prison when I was nineteen was like that. They took us to a cell house and posted each of us at different points, then left us alone with no radio, no panic button, and no officer to oversee what we did.

That sucked.

So I made sure to treat all my OJTs like they were part of the team and make myself available to offer guidance where I could.

A lot of the things they were told in training were not applicable in real life. It was one thing to act out little scenarios and read about what it was like behind the walls; it was quite another to actually experience it.

The OJT I had that day took forever to lock the guys up on her tier. Usually, when they first start, it takes a while to get a feel for the job. Plus every cell house is different because the people are different—inmates and staff.

But watching her, I realized what her problem was. It wasn't because she was petite or young. I'd seen women smaller than her with presence like a linebacker. No, she treated the inmates as if they had the right-of-way on the tier and they were walking all over her—almost literally.

I climbed the stairs to the tier and pulled her aside. "No, that's not how you do it."

"Well, I don't want to be rude, I want to build a rapport," she said eagerly.

I was heartened by how obvious she was about wanting to do a good job, wanting to be a good officer. "You know what kind of rapport you're building now? The bend-me-over-a-barrel-because-I'm-soft rapport. They don't respect you and they won't until you demand it."

"I understand I have to earn it."

"No, you don't. If you want to keep it, you have to earn it, but you're the officer. You're the one with the keys. You control movement, they don't. You control the tier, they don't. There is nowhere that they have to be that takes precedence over security. Security being you."

"They won't move," she said, hanging her head.

"It's your first day. It's okay. Listen to me, though; hold your head up. No matter what. Always meet their eyes. Looking away is an act of submission."

"God, like they're a pack of wolves of something."

"Yeah, just like that." I laughed.

"So, what if they won't move?"

"They'll move," I promised her. "C'mon. Walk the run with me."

I walked down the run with her behind me and without saying a word, every single inmate who was out for movement moved aside when he saw me coming. There were a couple cat-calls and instructions for me to train the newbie right, and a few telling her not to listen to me at all because I was too much of a hard-ass, but it was all light and the cell house ran smoothly.

When we walked back to the lockbox, she said, "That was awesome. I want to be an officer just like you."

Just like me? My first instinct had been to tell her, no, you don't want to be anything like me. But I couldn't help but feel proud that no matter what else I screwed up, this was something I could get right. This was something I was good at.

day 322

THE INMATES ALL KNEW I WASN'T RIPE FOR THE PLUCKING, but that didn't stop some of them from trying. I guess everyone loves a challenge.

There were some guys for whom telling them no didn't work, but they never crossed any lines where I could write them up. Being an annoying pain in my ass wasn't actually covered in the inmate rulebook.

In one cell house, this one guy would always find a reason to talk to me when I was posted there. He was never outright disrespectful, but he was like a fungus. Every time I turned around, he was there.

If he'd never done more than that, I probably wouldn't have been so irritated, but I could hear in his voice and infer it from some of the things he said that he thought if he could just put in enough time with me, he'd wear me down.

First, I tried laying it out for him. I told him that even if I wasn't married to another officer, I would never endanger my career or my coworkers that way. And all that aside, there was the fact that my father was a retired federal corrections officer, and he'd bury me in the basement with a ton of lime if he thought for one second I'd taken up with an inmate. He was also warned that if he pushed the issue he'd go to Seg. Well, he was one of those who liked to "winter" in Seg. As if it was some kind of vacation destination. He didn't mind it down there and he still had a lot of time left to do. So the usual motivators didn't apply.

I finally realized that I had to make him not like me.

But that was tricky too because I'd worked hard for my reputation. If I treated him badly, or any different than any other inmate, I wouldn't be a good officer.

I was talking to my second officer one day when he approached. She had brought me a root beer. He slid up to us, neat as a pin, and inserted himself right into the middle of the conversation as if we were at the food court at the mall instead of in a prison.

She looked at me and I looked at her—and some unspoken knowledge passed between us. She smiled and took a long gulp of root beer. Probably half the can. I did the same thing. He was still talking, the look on his face confident and his posture tall. He really thought he was getting somewhere.

He turned to say something else to me, and I burped. The biggest, loudest, lumberjackiest burp I could manage. If I'd been down in Seg, they would have given me a cookie and a that-a-girl slap on the back.

I think it may have actually *deactivated* the relaxer on his hair. He blinked against the onslaught and swallowed hard, obviously struggling. I had to give him credit, though, for not giving up. He turned to say something to my second officer as if my burp had never happened. I didn't offer an excuse me, a pardon me, nothing.

Then she responded in kind.

And hers was louder. In fact, I was pretty sure I could tell she'd had Chinese for lunch. Sweet and sour chicken and crab rangoon.

Not be daunted, he turned back to me and I took another long pull off my root beer. Upended the can.

"You might wanna take that a little bit slow, Sarge."

I smiled and burped again. I almost hurled because I had to dig deep for it.

"Aww, now you got somethin' somethin' too?" He turned back to my second officer.

She smiled again and lifted her leg. The eruption from her hind parts was so loud, I was sure that she'd shit her pants.

"You bitches is nasty," he said, shaking his head and stalking back down the run to his cell.

I laughed again, but then I was *sure* she'd had crab rangoon. We couldn't go back into the office for two hours.

It was worth it, though, because he never bothered me again.

There was another guy who I knew was jacking off every time I was in his cell house. That in itself isn't a big deal. It's prison. They're men. They're going to jack off, jerk the monkey, choke the chicken, burp the nephew, walk the purple-headed womb ferret, whatever. But this one would do it where he could watch me. He was a porter, and if he didn't watch me from his cell, he'd hide in supply closets. He'd stop when I'd walked by, so I had no reason to write him a disciplinary report. In prison, there are even rules about self-love and where and when it can occur. They have to be in their cells with a sheet over their bodies and no expectation of being viewed. So if he wasn't doing it when I was in front of his cell, he could argue that he had no expectation of being viewed.

If his constant onanism hadn't been aimed in my general direction, I wouldn't have fucked with him about it, but he was compulsive with it. I could tell just by the way he looked at me and every other female officer that he was a sex offender.

Yep. Three counts of rape.

So I decided I was going to break him of this habit.

What years of therapy couldn't do, humiliation would.

I put my plan in motion when I was in his cell house up on the second tier, helping the OJT officer lock up her inmates. They were running all over her like a parking lot. It was ridiculous.

I saw that the door to the supply/laundry room had been left open just a crack, and out of the corner of my eye, I could see this inmate inside. He was watching me.

And beating his meat.

So, when one inmate stopped to ask me something, I kept him there talking for a minute. Asked him about his day. I did that to get a feel for what was going on in the cell house. Other inmates saw this and wanted to talk too. So I waited until I had about ten inmates there waiting to ask me questions and then I flung the door open wide.

The offending inmate was standing there with his dick in his hand and about half a jar of Blue Magic hair pomade on his dick.

They all started laughing and pointing while he scrambled to pull up his boxers, slinging Blue Magic everywhere. A couple made comments about Smurfs jacking off and the laughter reached heights of hysterical.

"You're fucked up, Sarge," one of the inmates said to me.

"Why is that?"

"You knew what he was doing."

"I'm fucked up? I'm not the one with my dick in my hand," I snorted.

"If you don't want to see a man taking care of his business, you shouldn't work in a prison," he admonished.

"You don't want to be told when and where to take care of your business, you shouldn't come to prison."

"You got me there, Sarge. Yes, you do."

The inmate never bothered me again, and neither did any of the guys who were there for his humiliation.

day 325

I TALKED TO MY KIDS TODAY. I ASKED THEM TO FORGIVE ME and I promised them that from now on, no matter what happened, it would be better. That things would never be as they had been and I'd do everything in my power to make them happy.

They both fell into my arms and hugged me tight. I almost can't describe how I felt with their thin, little arms around me. It was warm like sunshine, bright with hope, and unconditional love.

I took them to the indoor pool at the community center and we saw an ex-inmate there. He wasn't one of the ones who just wanted to be validated. No, this one wanted to scare me.

We were the only ones there, swimming and splashing in the shallow end, when I decided to get out and relax on a lounger, just as if we'd been at an outdoor pool.

"Hey, Lunsford."

I looked up to see a big guy towering over me. He was inked from wrist to shoulder with gang tattoos, and his head had been shaved since last I'd seen him. But I recognized him from Seg.

"Hey, how are you?" I asked him, being cordial. As I said before, I usually wished them well when I saw them on the street. Or in this case, the pool.

I felt his stare on me, on my breasts in particular, like a ray gun. It was like he couldn't stare anywhere but there. Then I remembered he was a sex offender. I resisted the urge to pull my towel around me like armor. He'd see it as a sign of weakness, that his attention made me uncomfortable.

"You're looking really good," he said.

"Thank you." I made sure to look at his face and stare at him until he made eye contact and looked away. This tactic has worked for me with the majority of sex offenders I've worked with. Extreme scrutiny tends to make them almost bashful, but there are some, like this one, who remained unaffected.

He made the sound like sucking on his lips. "Damn, woman. Yes, you are."

"That's just as inappropriate here as it would have been behind the walls," I corrected him firmly but politely.

"I can't tell a bitch she's looking fine?"

"No, not when the bitch is married and has her kids. That's disrespectful. Especially in that tone, like I'm some ghetto rat ho. It would be the same as if I approached you while you were with your family and asked if you'd paid off your debt to the Latin Kings."

He laughed. "Still the same Lunsford, I see." Then he was quiet for a second. I really just wanted him to go away. "What about if it was in private? What about if I came to your house?"

"You aren't invited to my house. That would be inappropriate as well."

"I don't give a fuck about inappropriate."

"I do. So it was nice catching up. Good luck," I said, ending the conversation the same as I did with all of them.

Skeevy McSkeeverson didn't take the hint. Instead, he grabbed my wrist, hard. "I think I'm gonna come to your house anyway. Fuck you and those pretty girls of yours."

My children were still splashing and playing, oblivious to

what was happening. I could scream, but no one would hear me—there was no one else in the pool area. But I'm not the screaming sort anyway. I'm the rip-your-balls-off-and-shove-them-up-your-ass sort.

He squeezed my wrist harder, obviously trying to frighten me, and it hurt. It was my right wrist, I've broken it before. But I've also had two children without epidurals. This had nothing on that. Plus, it's always been my philosophy that pain is temporary and pride is forever.

Fuck him. He could snap my wrist and break my whole fucking hand off before he'd get a whimper out of me.

"Come to my house." I nodded. I even smiled. "I have two friends who would love to meet you."

He leaned down close in my face, still squatted down beside the lounger. "Oh yeah? What are their names, do I know them?" He leered at me.

I reached between his legs with my left hand and grabbed his balls as hard as I could and yanked him forward until I was right up in his face. "Yeah, motherfucker. You do. Smith and fucking Wesson. Come to my house, you sack of shit, and I'll feed this sad little lump of flesh to you one fucking bite at a time with a 12-gauge up your bitch ass."

"I could break your wrist," he said lightly, his voice a much higher pitch than it had been seconds before, refusing to acknowledge what I'd said. "I could choke you with my other hand and…"

I smiled again and he stopped speaking, obviously unsure of what to do with that big shit-eating grin on my face. "I don't give a fuck. Break it. It's been broken before." I twisted his balls a little harder, kept twisting until he yelped. "You stay away from my children, do you understand me? Threaten them again, so much as breathe in their general direction, and I will be your own personal hell on earth either until they find you in my basement or you die."

"I'm gonna call the cops," he whimpered.

"Call them. I don't give a fuck about that either. You just threatened my life and the lives of my children. You grabbed me. You just assaulted and battered a law enforcement officer. So go ahead and call whoever the fuck you think you want to call, and remember next time, if I pull a little harder, you'll be missing your balls. Now get the fuck out of here," I hissed when I let him go.

He stumbled backward and tripped over one of the other loungers.

"Momma, is that a friend?" my oldest called from the pool, having noticed the scuffle.

"No, that's not. If you see him again, yell Stranger Danger and run away as fast as you can."

"Is he a shit bag?" she asked.

One of our more colorful words for problem inmates. I sometimes forgot how sensitive their little ears could be. It seems they don't pay attention to anything you say until it's something you don't want them to hear.

But in this case, it was accurate.

"Yes, punkin. He is." I got out my phone and called the police to report the threat.

The responding officer laughed when he read my statement. I was honest about what I said to the inmate. I wasn't going to lie and say that I hadn't responded to his threats with some of my own. And as corny as it sounded, mine were promises. That piece of shit got anywhere near my kids, and I would have done every last thing I said I would do.

After all, I'm all about the follow-through.

day 328

WHEN I GOT TO WORK, THEY WERE SEARCHING EMPLOYEES on the way in.

We were searched every day before entering the facility, but this was more in depth. They had the drug dog out making the rounds.

This always made me nervous.

The apartment building where I lived was home to a bunch of degenerate fucks doing God knows what, and tracking it all over the place. Especially in the common areas.

One of the drug dogs had positively ID'd a friend of mine because she helped a friend who'd been a toker move, and they'd been in her car. Somehow, something had been transferred to her clothes.

She'd been stripped naked, had to endure a urinalysis, a blood test, and a cavity search. She had three days off that ended up being paid because everything came back negative.

I didn't fancy being naked in front of coworkers I wasn't fucking or having any one of them elbow deep in my vag. That did not sound like a good time.

My husband didn't give a shit. He said if they stuck their hand up his ass, they deserved whatever they got. He'd growl at the dog and try to get it to hit on him so he could get three days of paid vacation. Personally, I didn't think the extra leave was worth the whole experience of the cavity search.

The husband and I walked in together because we arrived for shift at the same time, and the first thing out of the dog handler's mouth was, "Lunsford, don't tease the dog." But he wasn't talking to me.

After the dog, we had a closer examination of our person and our belongings, going through stations: the dog would sniff us, then we'd go to have our belongings searched, then on to the next table for a physical, hands-on search of our person. I hated the pat-downs too because it tickled. I hate being tickled more than a yeast infection.

And it made me giggle.

Everyone always laughed at me on these search days and I went to my cell house feeling thoroughly tampered with.

It was for a good reason, though.

I got a call later because gossip always spread like wildfire. They'd caught a staff member bringing in contraband inside of what looked like sealed and unopened soda cans. It was no surprise to me.

I'd seen this staff member talking to inmates in the kitchen when I first started. She was being overly familiar with them, but everyone assured me I was confused about what I'd seen. So I went with the flow. I didn't say anything about it because I'd been fresh off the truck and I didn't want to make waves.

Dirty bitch.

One down and who knew how many to go?

A new shopping area opened up not too far from us, and one of the women who'd been fired for dirty bitchery got a supervisor position with their security company, which seriously made me question their background checks and hiring procedure. Anyway, before long, the entire place was staffed with prison rejects.

A couple officers came into my cell house one night and we were talking about what the hiring process must be like if they recruited straight from the prison's HR. "Here's your letter of termination and an application for…"

One of the women who'd been fired was pregnant with an inmate's baby. There'd be criminal charges following the paternity test because it's a sex crime to sleep with someone in your custody. Inmates can't legally consent to sex. And this place had hired her to see to the security of their center, made her responsible for shoppers, employees, property…Obviously she'd made such responsible choices.

One officer said she'd sent this woman a little striped outfit for her baby and had the inmate's number embroidered on the chest. She even sent a little hat. It looked like just the old-fashioned prison uniforms.

That made me laugh so hard, I almost peed my pants.

Maybe that sounds unreasonably cruel, but I thought it was kind, considering the ass kicking this bitch deserved. She put us all in danger because she couldn't keep her legs closed. Her pussy was more important than everyone else's life; that's what it boiled down to from our point of view.

Relationships between staff and inmates are dangerous because he'll either convince the staff member to bring in contraband, which leads to violence, or will perpetrate an act of violence on the staff member when the inmate stops getting what he wants.

Part of our job is the safety and security of the institution, and that includes all staff members. There isn't one good officer who wouldn't immediately launch themselves into the fray if they saw an inmate attacking another officer. Fights are never clean, and no one ever walks away unscathed. Any incident that involves the laying of hands of one party on another has the potential to escalate into a full-scale riot.

I know an officer who lost the use of his arm because he took a shank in it trying to save the life of another officer. She'd been sleeping with several different inmates and was bringing in drugs. When she got scared of the consequences and stopped supplying the inmate with sex and drugs, the inmate decided to teach her a lesson. He was going to kill her.

I still have the urge to trip her every time I see her and any other dirty bitch who could hurt the people I care about.

day 330

I'D BEEN IN CONTACT WITH AN EX-BOYFRIEND FROM HIGH school. A lot of my male friends were ex-boyfriends from one point or another. He was going through a divorce and having a really hard time. So we talked a lot, mostly online. I thought we'd really gotten to know each other again, and I was glad to count him as my friend.

He called me around midnight.

"Hey, Sara. Do you have some time? I really need an ear."

"Tough day?" I asked.

"Yeah, can I come over? I just…" he broke off.

He needed to talk. I understood. I'd been there. I still had days where I didn't know which way was up. It made me feel better about my own bullshit to help someone else with theirs.

"Sure, come on over." I didn't think anything of having someone over that late. The shift I worked didn't get over until ten; by the time everyone got home and ready to go do other things, it was usually eleven or twelve anyway. We were night creatures.

"I'll be there in five. I'm up the street at 7-Eleven. I just didn't have anywhere else to go."

"I know. It's okay. It'll get better, I promise."

"Thanks, Sara. I'll see you in a few."

It wasn't long before there was a knock on the door. I peeked out the window to make sure it was him and opened the door.

As soon as I opened it, the stench of Jack washed over me. He was drunk. He hadn't sounded drunk on the phone. Shit. I couldn't have that around the kids.

"Hey, man, you're drunk."

"Yeah," he agreed.

"That's not cool. You should have told me you'd been drinking. I could have gotten my friend to come over and watch my kids and I would have come to you."

"Yeah, well, I'm here now."

"Yes, you are. But you can't stay. I have my kids tonight. I don't want them to see you sloppy drunk. I've never been around them that way. Can I call you a cab?"

He didn't answer me, and I never saw it coming. For as careful as I'd been with who my children were exposed to, it had been a friend who was the predator. He punched me, his fist exploding in my face, and he knocked me backward—pushing his way into the apartment.

I ran through a gamut of emotion in seconds. Surprise, betrayal, pain, fear, and anger. I held on to the anger with both hands because I knew it could help me. I could feel the rest of it later after I handed him his ass on a platter.

"You fucking whore, taunting me, telling me to come over, now you tell me to leave. Fuck you, you'll give it up." He punched me in the face again.

I blocked the next blow, but he was stronger than me. So I tried to be faster, more cunning. I punched him in the solar plexus, dug my knuckles into him, but he kept coming.

But so did I. I went for his eyes, his throat, his knees, all the soft places that will bring a person down. I think he was on some kind of drug too because no matter what I did, he kept coming. I drew on all the things I'd learned at the prison, pressure points, things my husband had taught me on how to get out of different holds.

He slammed me down into the floor and although the sound echoed through the place like a gunshot, the sound of it barely registered. The heavy weight of him was like a brick wall, pushing me down, crushing me. I brought my knee up between us, but he clamped his thighs shut hard, holding my knee in place.

I bit his shoulder and cracked my head against his, aiming for the bridge of his nose, but I missed. He dragged me by the throat to the bathroom and slammed me against the wall, cracking my head against the mirror, shattered glass spraying from behind me.

It was then I realized how very loud we were. How the next sound could wake my children. I was struck by the thought of their sleepy little faces and the things they would see if they heard the noise and wandered out to see what was happening. I thought about my gun, and if I could get to it before he did. Where I should shoot him. Anywhere but in the chest or head and he could still keep coming. But if I killed him, I'd have to prove he was trying to hurt me, that I had a reasonable fear for my life.

What if he hurt my children? What if I missed or he got hold of my gun instead?

I'd kill him. I'd rip his fucking throat out with my bare hands if he hurt my kids.

But he'd still have hurt them. No matter what retribution I'd take, they would still have suffered.

I made the choice to stop fighting.

No matter what he did to me, it was better that he do whatever he felt he had to and leave than have anything happen to my children. Whatever he put me through would be worth keeping my children safe.

That's not to say I was a willing participant. "Please," I begged quietly. "Don't do this."

"Shut up, whore."

"Why do you want to hurt me? I'm your friend."

He kept tearing at my clothes; his big, sweaty hands were on my breasts. He squeezed them hard, bruised me.

"You want this, you fucking slut."

"No. I don't," I said quietly, fighting tears. I didn't want to cry, I was determined not to cry. "Stop. Please, stop." I hated how my voice shook with fear, I hated that I knew what he was going to do and how powerless I was to stop it.

I didn't fucking cry, but I couldn't get enough air to bawl if I'd wanted to.

He tore my pants down my hips, his hand still holding my wrists above my head and his weight locked me down beneath him.

"Remember when you said you loved me? When I loved you? If you ever loved me, you won't do this," I said quietly.

He didn't hear any of it, or if he did, he didn't give a fuck.

So instead, I looked at him. At his receding hairline, the puff of his fat cheeks as he worked against me, the hair on the back of his neck and shoulders. The smell of him, his sweat, the Jack, and some cheap Dollar Store aftershave. I studied each detail that disgusted me and told myself that this wasn't the end for me. This was happening to me, yes. But it would be over soon. My children would be safe.

And I'd go to the hospital, I'd file a police report, and then when he went to prison, I'd make sure whatever prison he went to, all of the officers there would know he'd assaulted one of their own. I'd make him pay for what he did to me.

He held me by my throat and tried to shove his dick into

me. He couldn't keep his dick hard, couldn't make it stand up and perform. Since he'd been my friend, listened to my hopes and fears the same as I listened to his, part of me hoped it was because he didn't really want to hurt me. Stupid, I know. Of course he did.

This person who'd once said he loved me, once promised me the moon and stars, when he couldn't keep his dick hard, he used his fist instead. He rammed his fist inside of me, his knuckles hard against my pelvic bone. I wondered if he'd fracture it. I'd started to go numb, but not before my perineum tore, just like when I'd given birth to my children. After I tore, he made some animal sound of pleasure. He was trying to ruin me, destroy that which made me a woman.

"Please stop," I begged again, trying to stay quiet.

"I'll stop when you scream," he said, like it was some kind of promise. Something I'd want.

Fuck you, motherfucker. You could set me on fire and I wouldn't scream now. My children would hear and I would be goddamned if I'd let that happen.

Since I dealt with sex offenders, I knew it wasn't about sex, what he was doing to me. It was about power. I wouldn't give that to him. Whether I screamed or not was still mine. He couldn't take that from me. So fuck him if I'd scream. Fuck him and his limp little dick.

My vision blurred, and I lost consciousness several times. He tightened his grip on my throat when I wouldn't scream. I tried to stay awake, even though part of me kept telling me to let go because when I woke up, it would be over. But I wondered if I passed out, if he would kill me.

Or if he got bored, if he'd find my kids and do this to them.

I almost didn't want to tell this part of the story. Again, for my children. I don't want them to read this and know what happened to me, to think what I suffered was in any way their fault. It's an ugly part of the world that I'd keep from them forever if I could. But when I started telling my story, I knew I had to show this too. It happens to thousands of women, and maybe my story could help someone else know they're not alone. Know there is life after someone does this to you and it can be a good life. A happy life.

He finally kissed me, his mouth heavy and wet—his tongue like a slug sliding between my lips.

"You're so beautiful." He kept kissing me and I thought about biting his tongue off, letting him slip it in my mouth and biting down as hard as I could, but I didn't. I don't know why I didn't. While he was squealing like a pig and bleeding, I could've bashed his head into the sink and done it until he was dead. Then he couldn't hurt me or my children. "Tell me, Sara. Beautiful Sara, tell me what you liked best so I'll know for next time."

I'm a writer. I should know the power of words. Here, these words, they were more powerful than any gun, any knife, even my teeth tearing out his tongue. They cut me so deep I couldn't answer him.

He kept petting my hair; I lay there, solid and still. A terror I'd never known before wrapped around me in the heaviest chains.

Next time? He could do this to me again? Like I'd asked for it? Like I'd invited it? Like I somehow deserved it? What I liked? I was nearly hysterical when I thought of it again, kept hearing it over and over in my head as I lay there.

He got up and pulled up his jeans, and left without another word.

I cried when the door closed. I sobbed into a towel, my head throbbing, my hands bloody from the glass, and more blood sticky down my thighs. I knew I had to get up. I had to get up then or I wasn't going to.

I wanted nothing more than to take a shower, to scrub his filth off me, to turn the water on so hot it would melt every bit of him off my skin.

But I didn't.

I cleaned up my face and my hands, rinsing away the blood and the glass I could get out myself. I knew since I'd scratched him, I shouldn't have washed them, but they were bloody. I didn't want my children to see. If they saw me like this...no.

So I put on a sanitary napkin and clean clothes. I balled my dirty clothes up and shoved them into a plastic bag. Then I sat down and waited until it was time to get them up for school. Even sitting there on the couch was sheer agony; it was like being stabbed with a knife between my thighs. When it was time, I got them dressed and I made them breakfast. I took them to school and tried not to flinch when they kissed my cheek a little too hard.

Then I went to the emergency room where I had to endure a rape kit and seven stitches where he'd torn me. I told them they wouldn't find anything. There weren't fluids because he hadn't been able to keep his dick hard, but I handed over the baggie of my clothes. I'd done everything right, except washing my hands.

The police came and the questions they asked me were almost as bad as the kit. Had we ever talked about sex? Did I invite him over for sex? Why would I let him in so late? Was I sure it was rape? Maybe I'd invited him over to fuck and had buyer's remorse. Because no woman who was raped would have the sense of self and presence of mind to bring her clothes.

I was so angry, but I answered their questions. I wanted to do this the right way. I wanted him to be punished so he couldn't do this to anyone else. I'd always prided myself on being strong, so now I had to prove it. I filled out my statement right there and signed it. It should have been easier from there.

But they didn't believe me.

I didn't act like a rape victim.

What does a rape victim act like? Is there a script? I know how to disengage my actions from my feelings. It's what made me a good officer.

So because I didn't lie down and fucking die, I must be lying? Since I didn't become agoraphobic and lock myself in my house, I'm lying? Since I wanted them to catch his punk ass and put him in prison, I was lying?

Motherfuckers. Every last one of them.

But I continued to answer their questions and jumped through all of their flaming hoops to file a report.

Weeks passed and when I never heard back, I went to follow up on my case. The officer I spoke to told me there was no record of any report and asked me if I'd like to file again.

It had been bad enough the first time, and since I had no record of my report, anyone who'd been inclined to believe me the first time wouldn't now.

At first, I was really angry about that. I felt incredibly wronged. Like someone owed me something for this. But I know how these things work in a small town. I resolved to let it go, at least the legal proceedings, but if he attacked me again, I'd kill him.

I was reminded of when The Old Man told me what a difference there was between saying and doing. It was my children that kept me from doing. I'd like to say I'm too good a person and I believe he'll be punished in the afterlife, blah blah. But I want him to be punished in this one. I want him to know what it's like to have his power taken away. To feel something trying to tear out his insides and telling him how pretty his suffering is and how much he likes it because he wanted that nightstick up his ass stirring up his guts.

But my revenge wasn't worth letting my children grow up without a mother.

Protecting myself was another story. If he came to my house again, I'd shoot him and deal with the fallout.

I wasn't going to tell anyone else what happened. What good would it do? They'd either see me as a victim or they wouldn't believe me. And either way, I had enough shit to deal with without other people judging me.

But I realized that was like lying.

So I told my mother, my husband, and a good friend. He wasn't my boyfriend yet; we'd talked about dating when my husband and I divorced.

My mother said that she'd always told me that someday, someone would be stronger than me. I don't think she meant it to be as shitty as it sounded, but it hurt. So I told her that all the time she'd smoked, I'd always told her she'd get cancer and hung up on her.

The future boyfriend asked me the same questions the police had, and to put the icing on that cake, in a later conversation he said that he'd talked to friends about what I'd said and that they were convinced I'd made it up for attention. That again, I didn't act like a rape victim.

That's because I'm not a fucking victim, cocksucker.

And how the fuck would they know? Have any of them been raped? And if they had, how could they say that about a woman they don't know? Everyone deals with trauma and pain in their own way.

How am I supposed to act? Never leave the house again? Cry? Stop eating? Stop going to work? Stop living? I won't deny I was screwed up, but how would any of that help me? The only thing it would do was give my rapist power over me. And I didn't let him have it while he was violating me, so why would I give it to him later? Fuck him. Fuck that. Fuck you.

I thank him for that now. For making me realize no one was going to get me through this but me. For making me see I had to stand on my own legs even if they were broken. And for making me see that he sure as hell wasn't the man for me.

But my husband? He just held me and told me it would be okay. That's all I wanted, and he just knew. He didn't make it about him, or about our relationship. For him, it was about me.

On one of our first dates, we'd gone to see *The Faculty*. One couple showed up throughout the movie and they were always pushing each other, saying, "Do something." And after the movie, we'd done the same thing to each other. It was a running joke. We used to wrestle around, spar and practice moves together. I discovered I couldn't do that with him anymore when I went over to his mother's house and we were talking and he nudged my shoulder. So, I nudged him back a little harder. "Do something," I demanded and laughed.

When he took me down, flattened me on the floor, I lost it. I don't remember what I did, but everything went black, and when I woke up, he was holding me, telling me his name over and over again, and promising it would be okay.

It was because of this incident that I sucked it up and went to a therapist that my psychiatrist friend recommended. I didn't want to be that woman, I didn't want my life or my relationships to be defined by what one person had done to me.

But it was a waste of my time.

I only went to one session and the therapist was a twat. She was so condescending, and when she asked me how something made me feel, I realized I couldn't pay a woman that stupid to be my friend. That's what therapy felt like to me. I was paying her to listen to me. How did that make me feel? Well, you stupid bitch, I was raped. How the fuck do you think that made me feel? What a stupid question.

I get that the point of therapy is to talk about your feelings and that's what I was doing. I didn't need to be prompted. I was spilling my guts, talking about my feelings, and then to ask me that dumbass question? Nope. I was done.

I'd dealt with everything else thus far on my own, so I'd deal with this too.

day 331

MY FIRST DAY BACK TO WORK AFTER IT HAPPENED WAS tough.

When the door clanged shut behind me in the sally port, I grabbed the edge of my coworker's jacket. Panic rose in my throat like bile. I hadn't told anyone else what had happened, so he asked me if I was okay and I nodded and let go. I acted like I was playing our usual game of trying to snatch something out of his pocket or his lunch box without him noticing. I'm sure he knew the difference; I'd never just grabbed his sleeve like some lost little kid. He let it go because he wasn't the type to pry, but he put his arm around my shoulder in a gruff hug to let me know he was there if I wanted to talk.

But I was okay. Not because he was there for me to grab his sleeve, but because I was going to make me okay.

The other door opened quickly and I was behind the walls.

I worried that they'd smell it on me. Like I was some gazelle who'd been culled from the herd and I was crawling on my belly through the savannah leaving a trail of blood behind me for the lions to follow. I didn't want to meet anyone's eyes. I thought for sure they'd see it if they couldn't smell it already.

But this was my job. No one was going to put food on my table but me. So I had to suck it up, pull up my big-girl panties and go to fucking work, and I couldn't act any different than I had before I'd been raped, or work would get a lot harder.

Once I was back in the cell house though, I found that if I didn't think about it, I could do it. I had the keys to the cages; I was the one in control. I was the one with the power.

day 340

ABOUT A MONTH AFTER IT HAPPENED, AFTER I WAS RAPED, I was in a cell house and an inmate tried to cow me. He got very angry with me because I wouldn't let him use the phone. He was on restriction, which meant no phone privileges. He wanted to call his daughter on her birthday. But I'd already seen this asshole's file. He was in prison for molesting her. I'm sure a call from him was the last thing she wanted on her birthday.

He tried to act like he wasn't going to go to his cell after I'd told him no. He said I was messing with the wrong man. The same overused, overtired litany of shit I heard day in and day out. He stepped into my personal space while he was yelling, and I wrapped my fingers around my radio ready to crack him in the head with it. I didn't back down. I thought for a moment I was going to have to call an alarm, but he stepped back and went to his cell when he saw I wasn't intimidated by him.

Later in the night when I was running doors to let guys out for religious callouts, he crept up behind me. I still don't know what his intentions were; he swears he was just trying to talk to me, but everyone in prison knows better than to sneak up on an officer or even another inmate. Further, inmates and officers both keep a reasonable, professional distance from each other unless direct contact is necessary.

I don't know if I felt his presence, if some sound alerted me to him, but I knew I had to fight. I didn't even take the time to turn around before I engaged. I stepped back hard on his instep, brought my elbow back with all the force I could manage into his gut, and spun around and shoved him as hard as I could to put as much distance between us as possible. It was a move for my safety and also so I could analyze the threat and have a few more seconds to decide my next action.

He lay on the ground where he'd fallen and put his hands behind his back to be cuffed. At that point, my second officer should have called an alarm, but he didn't. He didn't do anything but stand there slack-jawed and stupid. I had to tell him to go finish letting inmates out for callout and locking up those who'd returned.

I could have called an alarm here as well, but I didn't think the situation warranted it after I already had the cuffs on him. I walked him to the office and called the Captain to let him know what happened.

The inmate ended up staying in my cell house rather than going to Seg, and I was okay with that. We'd each made our point and my dick was bigger. He was just a bully who thought he could intimidate me into giving him his way.

day 343

I HAD SEX AS SOON AS MY STITCHES HEALED.

Sex had always been a good part of my relationship with my husband, even when we were separated. We couldn't keep our hands off each other.

I remember one night before this happened. He came into work and was on his way to his post when it just struck me how absolutely delicious he was. I passed him on the yard, and I couldn't help but drag my hand over his shoulder and bicep. He was so strong and tall—formidable.

He has this thing he does when he's in a situation where he needs to make it clear he's the alpha male. It's not even a conscious thing, but he swells. He puffs up like a blowfish. Everything on him gets bigger. He gets measurably taller, his muscles flex, and he carries himself in such a way that makes him look bigger too. It's sexy as hell.

I would have dragged him out into the parking lot if I thought I could've gotten away with it. He knew too. That's something else about my husband, he's so confident. Sometimes it comes off as arrogance, but he wears it well.

I needed that strength again when I decided I wanted to have sex. I knew it would be with him, whether or not we got back together. He was the only one I trusted with that.

Logically, I knew he wouldn't hurt me. I knew sex didn't have to hurt and it wasn't about pain. One man had done something bad to me, but it was my body and I was going to use it as I saw fit. I'd enjoyed sex before and I wasn't going to let him take that away from me either.

So I told my husband what I wanted. He didn't ask me if I was sure, didn't ask me if I wanted to talk about it, or pick it to death like some rancid scab. He just accepted what I said and came over.

He brought me a rose and rented a movie. It was almost like when we were dating. I can't count how many movies we rented, starting watching, but never got more than ten minutes into because we always ended up naked.

The first time he kissed me that night, I wanted to scream. When I closed my eyes, I saw my attacker. So I kept my eyes open. It was a little weird to kiss him with my eyes open, but it was irrefutable truth the man kissing me was my husband. The man's hands on my body belonged to him. I wanted them there; I'd invited them to be there.

It still hurt like a motherfucker.

It was like I was a virgin again. I didn't tell him that though. And I think he deserves a whole box of cookies for not being weirded out when he opened his eyes and saw my eyes were open and knew they had been the whole time.

He just accepted that as what I needed to get through this.

It was completely unexpected how considerate and tender he was. We'd never been like that in bed. It was always intense and all about building the physical feeling. It was never slow, patient, and gentle.

When we'd split up, we didn't even like each other. I'd felt nothing but relief that he was gone, but now I only felt that relief when he was close to me. He asked me if it hurt and I said no. I didn't want him to stop.

I was going to take my life back and nothing was going to stop me.

I FINALLY TOLD SUNSHINE WHAT HAD HAPPENED.

She told me she was proud of me, for how strong I was to be moving on with my life. She didn't say she was sorry for what had happened to me, she didn't treat me like a victim. And she asked me if she could share something with me.

Whenever she'd offered advice in the past, it was never what she would do in the situation. It was what she thought I should do. What would be best for me, not what would appease her ego. So I said yes, that I was ready to hear it.

Sunshine told me I could choose happiness. That was the best thing of all—it was within my power. It wasn't some dancing butterfly to flit away from me, but it was heavy and solid. Something I could decide to hold onto, and it started with being thankful.

We'd had this conversation before, but I hadn't been ready to hear what she had to say. While it began identical to the previous conversation, the place we ended up was completely different.

I asked her what if I didn't have anything to be thankful for, and she said I just wasn't looking hard enough. To start small. With something seemingly insignificant. To take something I was unhappy about and find the good in it. When she couldn't find a job, she said she was thankful for the desire to work. Something so tiny, but it led to other things. Yes, Sunshine had said this before too. I'd tried it, and it had worked. But with this? It couldn't possibly.

I started with being thankful for the desire to be happy. It's a small thing, and you'd think everyone has it, but they don't. Not actively. When I was face down puking canary yellow mixed drinks out of my nose like some tropical island fountain? I didn't have that then.

Then I was thankful for my friend, for her lessons that brought her the knowledge to share with me. I was thankful that I wanted to be a better person. I was thankful for the width and breadth of the hearts of the people I loved and that they could forgive me. I was thankful for the story idea brewing in my head because I knew I was going to write again.

She was right. Happiness was just like misery. It would build on itself over and over again until you had a pile of shit or a pearl. Finally, as my awareness of my blessings kept building, I started crying again. But this time, it was because I was happy. I'd built my joy to such fervor that when I finally got to the big blessings like my family and my friends, I was overwhelmed with the sheer beauty of everything. It was like another kind of high, but it was healthy and good.

It gave me hope that I hadn't just been blowing smoke up my own ass and everything really would be okay—better than okay.

Even after everything, I could be happy.

day 345

SMALL SPACES WERE NOT THE PROBLEM, SO IT WASN'T claustrophobia in the traditional sense. It was any space I didn't have control over. Since the sally port had bothered me, I wondered if I'd be okay in the tower. The towers were small. Enclosed.

But I had control over my space, over entry and exit. Unlike the sally port, where someone else controlled the gates.

That's always been one of my biggest triggers, the loss of power. Only now, it was magnified ten thousand percent.

I've had a harder time coming to terms with my debilitating and gut-wrenching terror at being confined to any space that resulted from the rape than I do with the rape itself. Yes, he took my power away by raping me, by forcing me to submit to a physical act that was unwanted. But the fact he was in my head, that I allowed him to be in my head, that was the cardinal sin. Because I was supposed to have control of myself. I choose my actions. I choose my reactions.

But I didn't choose. I was being swept away by this tidal wave of fear and that was so far beyond unacceptable to me. I'd always been fearless, strong, armored in a sense. I was the one who always had an answer and a safe, warm place beneath her wing for those who weren't as strong as I was. Craven weakness had always disgusted me more than stepping in a pile of warm dog shit with bare feet, and now I was the one with broken wings out in the cold.

I know some people would say it wasn't weakness, that I needed time to heal, that my reactions in the situation were perfectly normal. Maybe they were. For other people. Not for me. I'm the one who ran down Independence Avenue in my bare feet after my ex-boyfriend chased me with an axe and laughed about it later with the Mexican gang members who saved me. I'm the one who was a single mother who went back to work two weeks after my daughter was born to take care of my responsibilities. I'm the one who stood between a friend and her abusive shit-bag ex when she finally decided to leave him and when he took a swing, he was the one who got his ass kicked in the most cliché way possible, a dirty frying pan on the stove. That was me. This sniveling, needy, *broken* thing was not.

But it was.

And I hated it. I was so disgusted by myself. More so than even with the drinking because when I realized I was self-medicating with the alcohol, I just stopped. I said I was going to quit and I did.

I guess my mother was right and someone was, finally, stronger than me.

day 346

WHILE ON SOME LEVEL I KNEW MY HUSBAND AND I WERE going to work it out when in the middle of Best Buy he pulled me close to him and we started dancing to Etta James, I hadn't been ready for it then.

I wasn't ready to acknowledge it until the night I came home from work and he was waiting for me in my apartment. That was the reason I didn't want him to have a key to start with, but I found I couldn't be angry with him for being there, even though I wanted to be.

We finally talked about everything. He admitted who he'd slept with and I admitted who I'd slept with. Then it got ugly. All the confession wasn't good for the soul; it just hurt. We said some horrible things to each other. I guess to really take you there, I should describe them. Tear the hole wide so you can see everything, but it's not just about me and I don't want him to look like any less the knight in shining armor he is now. It's okay if you know what an asshole I was because that's mine to tell.

But the details of what was said don't really matter. What matters is when everything was said and done and he was ready to walk out my door for what would be the last time, I couldn't let him go.

I asked him to stay.

He said only if he was staying for real. Only if he could move in. Only if we were together.

I said yes.

In two weeks, we had the kids living there with us too.

It was a shitty one-bedroom matchbox, but it was ours. We were together.

Boy, were we together. We gave the kids the bed and we slept on a broken-down futon. Once we lay down for the night, that was it. There was no wiggling, no stretching, no turning over. We were forced to sleep snuggled up together. That wasn't something we'd ever done before. If we didn't keep all the weight in the middle, the leg would collapse.

We'd fall asleep all cuddled up together in front of the tiny TV with a movie on we'd all seen before. I remember those as some of the happiest times we've ever had.

day 347

I TOLD MY FRIENDS THAT MY HUSBAND AND I WERE BACK together. I shouldn't have been surprised by their reactions, but I lost even more friends than when I quit drinking.

A couple told me they were happy for me and wished us the best. Others asked if it was a wise idea. Others still kept telling me my husband was still sleeping with this woman and that woman, but they were saying the same things about me, and they were patently untrue.

Even the inmates knew what was going on, and some congratulated me. Others said we deserved each other because we were both the meanest and most awful people they'd ever met in their lives.

As much as I tried to leave our personal shit at home, it followed us behind the walls. Either because inmates heard us talking or officers talked to inmates about other officers' business. Like the woman (another officer) he'd been spending time with. She spilled her guts all over the place. Told every inmate who would listen about her would-be relationship with my husband, and how she planned to get me out of the picture.

The funny thing was this inmate she'd confided in, he'd asked me if I wanted him to take a shot at her. He said she was a dirty whore who'd never get enough dick and put us all in danger. He didn't like the idea of her trying to screw with my life and my career. He said he had no respect for her.

I told him no, that no matter what she'd done, she was still an officer and not to talk that way because I'd have to turn him in.

And he said he should have known better than to ask, apologized for putting me in that position, and said that was part of why he respected me so much.

day 350

THIS PART MAY BE THE HARDEST FOR ME TO WRITE. To admit to. Not being a shitty mom, a shitty daughter, or a shitty wife. Not even being raped. I owned all of those things. Even with the rape, I did have a choice. Choosing my children's safety over my own didn't feel weak. But this…it makes me feel so naked.

Exposed.

You know those stupid online memes where they ask you a million getting-to-know-you questions? When it comes to "biggest fear" I never answer it. Admitting I'm afraid of something is like pulling off my skin so all my nerves are exposed, and rubbing them with sandpaper. If I tell anyone what I'm afraid of, they can use it against me. Back to the loss of power. So that made what happened all the worse.

But I promised myself I wouldn't half-ass it. I've bled all over these pages this far, I'm not going to stop now.

I came into work like any other day, and there was a different Captain on shift. One I hadn't worked with before. Well, that's not exactly true. I'd had one run-in with him before. When I was new on shift, I'd been assigned a post where the officer had to come in two hours early. Whoever was in charge of scheduling was supposed to call me or send me some notification of the post. That didn't happen. Control called me a half an hour before shift started when they realized the oversight. I said I'd make it as soon as I could.

When I came through the gates, the regular officer assigned to the post on the first shift was already leaving. *Without being properly relieved.* I was only three minutes late. They didn't even pay overtime until seven minutes after the hour.

I was standing in the sally port, the small space between the sets of gates, waiting for the other gates to open, and a man stood there giving me a shitty look. He had his name on his shirt, but he was wearing a polo. Not the BDUs that had rank insignia on the collar. Although, I have to say, that probably wouldn't have mattered if I had known who he was. He was a raging cock.

"You're late."

Really? I didn't know that. Thanks for clearing that up.

"The post is unattended and that's unacceptable. You're probably going to get a write-up."

A write-up for something that wasn't my fault? If it was my fault, fine. But someone else had dropped the ball and I had hauled ass in to cover. So a write-up? A stain on my record that would affect my promotability? Fuuuuck you. "What's unacceptable is whoever the dumbshit was who let him leave without being properly relieved. Or whoever didn't give me twenty-four notice of my change in shift like they're supposed to. That's what's unacceptable."

"Do you know who I am?" he snapped, like he was someone famous and I should be licking his ass and calling it caviar.

I almost said I didn't give a shit, but considering where we were and the time, I assumed he was probably brass. I wasn't going to back down now. If he was the one who let the other officer go early, he was the one who was wrong. So I shrugged dismissively.

"Can't say that I do. And like you said, I'm late." I pushed through the door into the Max and went to my post. I found out later he was the Captain.

And I'd called him a dumbshit. Great. But honestly, and I say again, he was the one in the wrong and I'm not going to take an ass-chewing or a write-up that I didn't have coming.

So he'd just come to our shift, and when he started announcing post assignments for the day, a brick settled in my gut. I knew he was going to give me the shittiest thing he could find. He gave me an entry/exit point in the middle of the institution. A place where staff and inmates could pass between the Max and the Medium. It was where inmates entered and exited the institution. It was where staff turned in and exchanged equipment. It was a big, fat pile of shit. I could have gotten over that. Shit I could handle. The part where it was in a tiny, dark room no bigger than a bathroom was what I couldn't handle. Added to that was that the only way I could get in or out of this tiny room was with two keys. One person on the outside and me on the inside both turning keys. If there was a fire, any officer inside would be fucked face down like a dead whore in the back of a Lexus.

I'd be trapped.

I waited until everyone left to their assignments and I approached the Captain privately.

"Captain, sir?"

He looked down his nose at me, like I knew he would, but the fear of that small room was stronger than my pride. "Can I please be assigned to another post?"

He laughed as if I'd asked him if he'd give me a million dollars. "No, girl. We're short-staffed. I don't have anyone else who's done the post before."

"I haven't either, really. I trained in there for three hours. I don't know what I'm doing."

"You will after tonight."

"I can't." I shook my head. "Please put me somewhere else. I'm claustrophobic and—"

"We don't have time for this. Go to your post."

So I did.

I told myself that I could do this. It was part of my job. I *had* to do it. I thought about going home sick, but then I got really pissed off at myself for even thinking it. *Go to fucking work. Pay your bills. Put food on the table and quit fucking whining.*

Fear coiled like a serpent around my guts as I walked across the facility to my post. My hands started shaking and I felt those tremors through my whole body.

It's just a fucking room, I told myself. There's nothing in there that can hurt me. It's just…stuff and paperwork. Nothing to get my knickers in a wad over.

I felt like some kid afraid to look under the bed, but rather than fearing what could possibly be under there, I knew the exact nature of the beast. It was a golem of memory dredged up from hell that would close off my air and my senses until all I could do was relive those moments, that helplessness over and over again.

The building loomed before me, somehow bigger and darker in my dread. The gates like some hallway to hell.

I can't express how much I hated myself in that moment. Even my disgust at my reaction wasn't enough to drown out the fear, although it propelled me forward anyway. My instincts demanded I run in the other direction and never look back.

My common sense told me to stop being a pussy and do my damn job.

As I watched the key turn in the lock, I thought I was watching a Sword of Damocles slicing ever closer to my throat and the other officer smiled at me kindly. She'd seen plenty of first-timers to the post awash in trepidation.

When I stepped into that dark, tiny space, it hit me in the face with a sledgehammer. The smell of *him*. The weight of *him*. My head cracking the glass of the mirror. His hands on me. I wanted to fucking scream, but I couldn't get enough air in my chest to make a sound. Then that door slammed behind me and the key twisted in the lock, bolting me inside.

Bile rose in my throat and I swallowed hard. Like the simple act of swallowing could push down the fear, the disgust, and the memory. Even talking about it now, I want to vomit and cold fingers are digging into my shoulders, spiders skittering up and down my spine. I want it to stop, but we've come this far. I can do this. I'm stronger now. I've already survived this, so there's nothing more to be scared of, right? I'll call my critique partner and cry after the chapter is done, but it'll be good. A release. And she'll tell me it's okay and I know that it really is.

With one other officer in there with me, it wasn't so terrible. I didn't feel trapped. So I sat in the corner and quietly started putting equipment away in the cubbies that were specifically labeled for equipment for each person. The monotony of the task made my brain shut down; the memories faded, and by the time I'd put everything away, I thought it would be okay.

Until the other officer left and I was alone.

God, the sound of that door when it clanged shut was always heavy, but this was like some great satanic bell tolling in the dark.

I sat down at the desk, hands shaking, and tried to do my job. I had to monitor inmate movement, staff movement, and nine doors I had to use to process this movement. It was a busy time of day, but I couldn't concentrate on what I was supposed to be doing. I could barely concentrate on breathing, let alone higher brain function.

The room seemed smaller, darker. He lived in the shadows and he was there with me. His hand on my throat again, the ripping sensation of his fist inside me. His whiskey breath in my face. That wrecking ball of memory slammed into me over and over again, harder and harder, and there were some moments when I wasn't sure what was real and what was recall.

To my absolute shame, tears gathered and burned down my cheeks. I remember thinking they were like acid. I tried to keep up with what was going on outside, tried to do my job, but I couldn't. Not reliving that over and over again. I couldn't breathe. I couldn't think. All I could do was remember.

I managed to call the Captain. I told him I was sick and I had to go home. He told me that the staffing situation hadn't changed and I wasn't allowed to leave.

That was the nail in the coffin. *I had no control.* I was locked in a little black room with my terror, and he wouldn't let me out. I begged him. I was sobbing hysterically. He hung up on me and left me there alone with my demons.

All I could do was cry. Inmates and staff were pressing their faces up against the window and I sank to the floor. I had to get away from them, from the accusation I saw in their eyes, the glee, or even, in some cases, concern. I had to hide. I didn't want anyone else to see me. Everyone would already know that I'd cracked, had some kind of meltdown. But they couldn't see this. Then everyone would know I was weak, helpless. That I was prey—a victim. I crawled under the desk and sobbed.

The phone kept ringing, the buzzer kept ringing for staff to be let through the gates, and I couldn't do anything. I was paralyzed—my fingers wouldn't move. I was rooted in place like some heavy chains had been wrapped around me. I was drowning in terror.

I had a gun. I wildly thought about shooting my way out, but I had enough sense to remember that the glass was bulletproof and I'd probably just end up shooting myself. And it briefly occurred to me that if I did shoot myself that this would stop.

This would all end and he'd never be able to get to me again. It would be over.

That thought was a smack to the face, not quite like the sledgehammer, but it was just as jarring. I didn't want to die. I just wanted it to stop.

I finally reached up and answered the phone. It was another officer who'd already heard that I was losing my shit, and she asked if I was okay. I told her I was definitely not okay and I needed to go home. She said she'd call the Captain for me.

I stayed under the desk.

The Captain called me back and said he was sending some-one to help, but I still couldn't go home.

When the yard officer came to help me, he stayed in be-tween me and the door until it had been secured. Another officer turning the key to lock us both in. He'd been instructed not to let me out.

I don't know if the Captain was trying to teach me something or if he thought I was being a drama queen, but he wasn't going to let me out until shift was over. Hell or high water. Bastard.

I think if I'd fought him, the other officer, I could have gotten out. The other officer was smaller than me and I had a gun. But I wasn't in my right mind. I was still half-frozen and out of my head with fear. It didn't occur to me then that I could have pushed past him and gotten out. I was too lost in that haze of terror.

Crumpled up on the floor, I kept bawling and the other officer did my job. He handed me tissues every once in a while, but other than that, he ignored me until he had to leave. He didn't ask what happened, didn't ask if I was okay. I think if I'd stopped breathing, he probably would have stepped over me and gone about his business.

By eight o'clock, I'd been in Hell for five hours and it finally sank into my brain that I couldn't leave. No matter what I did. That surrendering to this fear, this terror, wasn't helping me, and if I could just make it another two hours, I could go. It would stop. I'd never have to come back.

So when the other officer left, I got up and I did my job. I stopped crying. I didn't have any tears left to cry anyway. He was still there, my rapist. I could feel his breath on the back of my neck, his glee at my pain and fear, but I knew it wasn't real. And if it had been, there was nothing I could do to change it anyway. All I could do was suck it the fuck up and do my job for two hours. Just two hours.

I ran a paper towel under cold water and put it on my face and made myself breathe and forced myself to go through the motions until my relief arrived.

When the door opened and I could leave, I was afraid of that too. Almost like I thought if I went through the door, someone would make me go back inside. I kept thinking someone was going to stop me as I was leaving.

I finally exited the institution out into the parking lot, and the cool night air chilled my tear-streaked and swollen face. Breaths came deep and slow, filling my lungs, and I concentrated on the simple pleasure of that—inhale, exhale, inhale... The repetition was soothing, calming. I don't think I've taken such joy in the simple act of breathing. Then I saw my husband in the car waiting to pick me up. I almost fainted with relief. Or at least I think that's what fainting would feel like; I've never fainted in my life, but my knees were weak and I felt bone-less, exhausted, and like my consciousness was hanging on by a thread. Darkness hovered at the edges of my vision and it wasn't scary like the dark inside that room, it was warm, comforting, and safe.

When I got inside the car and saw my husband, I knew I didn't need the darkness. I was safe. He'd never let anyone or anything hurt me like that again. If I'd had tears left, I would have sobbed more with relief. My husband took one look at my face and immediately demanded what the fuck? I asked him to just drive, to get me away from there. So he did and I told him what had happened. He said I never had to go back if I didn't want to. That I should quit and pursue my writing full time and that he'd get a second job again and that everything would be okay. He'd take care of me.

But I didn't want to quit. Even after losing my shit all over the place like some little girl afraid of the dark. Even knowing that everyone would know, that I'd get a healthy ration of shit from everyone who could remember that day for the rest of my career.

I liked my job. I was good at it. Yes, I wanted to write full time. What writer doesn't? But corrections was something to do that I could be proud of to pay the bills until my writing took off.

I'd made a total ass of myself, but that was distant to every-thing else. I decided to go to my doctor and get a note for a medical leave of absence so I could think about my options.

day 351

I BAWLED AGAIN WHEN I TOLD THE DOCTOR WHAT HAPPENED. I was so embarrassed and disgusted with myself. She held my hand and listened. Then she wrote an excuse that said I was medically unable to work until further notice so I'd have all the time I needed to decide what else to do.

She also asked me if I needed any antidepressants or if I needed something to help me sleep. I confessed my drinking and I told her I didn't want to medicate myself anymore. She understood, but made me promise that if things got bad, I'd come back in.

Spent the rest of the day with my kids. I took them to their favorite restaurant with animatronic dinosaurs and then we went walking by the river. I wanted to cry again, just watching them. It occurred to me that I had this second chance to be their mom. To be good at it.

I knew working at the prison wasn't conducive to that. Not the shift I was on or the person I was when I was working there. The person I had to be behind the walls.

I'd take the rest of the time I had to think about it, but I'd known somehow when I left that day, I'd never go back inside as an officer. I'd broken like a rotten board. No matter the reason, I was damaged goods.

After the kids went to bed, I turned on my desktop and I

opened a blank Word document and I started writing. It was a story about a witch who'd summoned a demon to get rid of her Russian mobster ex-boyfriend. The demon who became the hero sounded a lot like my husband in my head.

day 364

I WENT INTO HUMAN RESOURCES TO TALK TO THE MANAGER about my job. Part of me had accepted I'd never be going back, but there was still part of me that didn't want to be told I couldn't. I was still trying to hang on because I knew I'd passed my first year and I was afraid I wouldn't be good for anything else but corrections.

After telling my story to the human resources manager, she said she sympathized with my plight, but there couldn't be any post I wouldn't work if I wanted to keep my job. I offered to surrender my rank and take a demotion if I never had to work that post again. She said no.

I asked her about the disabled people we had working there. There were officers there who couldn't do lots of things: some with pacemakers, with prostheses, all manner of disabilities. I was fucking raped. How did that not qualify for some leeway too?

She told me again if I couldn't do all the posts, they didn't want me. So I turned in my resignation.

And I was pissed.

I considered writing a letter to the warden, copying it to the Secretary of Corrections. I considered contacting activist groups. I even considered suing. I talked to a lawyer who told me I had one hell of a case.

I said I was sick and had to go home. They couldn't lawfully keep me there. The lawyer told me to go down to the police station and file charges for kidnapping because they'd held me against my will for eight hours and tortured me by keeping me in a place that terrified me.

She was convinced I could even get a nice settlement for pain and suffering.

Maybe some people will think I was stupid for not pursuing my case, but I didn't want that. I just wanted my job. Until then, I was a good officer.

And my husband, he was still employed there. He loved his job too. I couldn't take that away from him. If I sued, they would have made his life a living hell. He wouldn't have complained, he would have sucked it up and gone to work anyway. Until they found some reason to fire him. No, that's the hand that still feeds my table and I'm smart enough not to bite it.

I thought about all the energy that goes into a case like that and I didn't want to dwell on it, to wallow around in it like some pig in slops and hang myself up on the cross like some victim. I wanted to live my life. I wanted to be a good mother, a good wife, a good daughter. Those things were more important to me than vindication or validation. I survived it. Just like everything else that had punched me in the balls. What was the use in hanging on to it and letting it fester like some infection?

So I let go.

I let go of The Job, I let go of my rage, and I let go of my expectation that I was owed something for what I'd been through. The world didn't owe me anything. Bad things happen to people all the time. Good people. Bad people. People.

But I could choose to be happy. I could choose to move forward rather than live in the past. I realized sometimes it takes more strength to let go than to hold on. It would have been easier to be pissed off, to have someone else to blame. A target for everything that hurt. Or I could file it away with everything else that had happened to me, pull up my big-girl pants, and choose what I would take from life rather than what it would give me.

So when I walked out of the building that day, the sun was shining bright on my face and I inhaled deeply, the air filling my lungs, expanding, pushing them as far as they could go. When I exhaled, it felt like I hadn't been holding my breath for just that second, but for years. It was more than carbon dioxide spilling from me, but everything bad, everything rotten. I decided to leave my baggage at the gate. For real this time. I wouldn't be picking it up again.

I was done.

day 365

IT WAS BARELY DAWN AND THE LIGHT WAS SOFT SLIPPING through the gaps in the shades and the curtains to halo my whole world in a glowing, gold nimbus. My children, sleeping peacefully, their deep, even breaths a comfort—their skin perfect and smooth in the gentle light. My oldest daughter was tugging on her ear as she slept and my little one was curled into her. They looked like puppies that had been roughhousing and dropped where they stopped.

My husband was sleeping next to me, low rumbling in the back of his throat like some wild animal, but even that was dear to me. Even so, I still pinched his nose closed for just a moment so he'd roll over. If I hadn't, I knew his throat would be sore when he woke up.

I breathed again.

It's a simple thing, the mechanics of breath. The inhale, expanding, absorbing. The exhale, contracting, and expelling. I'd experienced the first taste of this on my escape from the room, and at the time, I'd never thought breathing could feel so good. Yet, this was even better; it was like decadence. It had never felt like happiness.

"Thank you," I whispered quietly. For my breath. For the sun on my face. For my children, for my husband, for the power to choose.

And then I rolled over and pressed my face against my husband's back, burrowed against the solid wall of him, his strength, and went back to sleep simply because it felt so good.

For all that I'd been through, I had this absolute surety that I was finally exactly where I was supposed to be.

afterword

I HAVE SO MUCH TO BE THANKFUL FOR, I DON'T EVEN NEED to start with the little things anymore and work my way up, although I am thankful for them as well. Sometimes the little things can be the biggest of all. I am thankful for everything that brought me to this place in my life.

Even the hard, ugly things that are difficult to talk about. They forged me; they forced me to learn lessons that I needed before I could move forward with my life. They taught me how to let go of rage and pain. How to find the joy in life when it seemed there wasn't any. They taught me how to love someone more than myself, how to be a good mother, a good wife, a good daughter, and a good friend.

I also believe that some of these things had to happen to me because I'm strong. Not to break me, but because I'd come out the other side still swinging and I can share that with someone else who might not have the same armor I do. Knowing that my rapist might read this and know he got into my head, that's a nasty feeling. Another violation, but fuck him because it'll be worth it to know that maybe my voice touched someone else and let them know they're not alone and there is life—good life—after rape. Or any other dark things that have touched their lives. It doesn't have to define you. You define you.

In all the best stories, Happily Ever After is only earned

through blood, sweat, tears, and sacrifice. So, for all the horror and darkness, I wouldn't change anything. My life has been like a really good romance novel. Or at least the ones I like to read and write. There's action and adventure, a spunky Amazonian heroine, and a handsome hero who is in just as much need of saving as the heroine. They both face internal and external dark forces, find their redemptive arcs, ride to each other's rescue, and love conquers all.

And I lived Happily Ever After.

glossary

bean hole: an opening in the cell door where food and other items are passed to the inmate; in times past, chow usually consisted of beans, hence the moniker

blacksuits: a special crew of officers who were supposed to be our elite; the guys we called when things got rough

Blue Magic: a brand of conditioner and hair pomade that is used for lube; at one time, the name also meant a kind of heroin, but in prison, it's fast and easy lubrication for anal penetration

brass: high-ranking officers

chester: child molester

contraband: any unauthorized item or an authorized item that has been altered from its original purpose that can induce harm

cred: credibility

crunch: canteen items, food stuffs

diaper sniper: child molester

dirty bitch detector: that seemingly supernatural awareness that another officer is either bringing in contraband or riding the baloney pony with an inmate or four

fishing line: something the inmates use to "fish" to get a kite or other contraband into their cells; can be made of bed sheets and a pencil, twine, thread, or even garments

flag: the ground floor of a cell house

hepatitis: a nasty disease that involves liver failure

hooch: homemade (vomit) liquor

house: cell

kite: note to one inmate from another or from a snitch to an officer

MRSA: antibiotic-resistant poop bug

OIC: officer in charge

PC: pussy control (okay, not really); protective custody

plug: something packaged to fit in the prison wallet

prison purse: vagina

prison wallet: anus

run: another name for tier or a level of cells

sally port: a small controlled space with two doors; you must pass through one door and secure it before passing through the second

scabies: itchy little bugs that build warrens under your skin and itch like the wrath of God

shank: homemade knife

shes: male inmates who carry themselves as women

skank: see dirty bitch detector

snitch: rat, someone who talks to the police

street: the pavement between cell houses, i.e., the Max Street or the world outside the walls

taco: vagina or man-taco (the anus); can be a feminized reference to "junk"

tier: a level of cells

tower rat: an officer who rarely comes out of the tower to work the ground or a cell house

about the author

S ARA LUNSFORD WAS A SEGREGATION OFFICER AT AN ALL-
male maximum-security facility and was promoted to the
rank of sergeant before leaving corrections to pursue a full-
time writing career. Sara's fiction has been published under
pseudonyms in magazines, anthologies, and novel-length
work. She lives in Kansas.